RESCUE BELOW ZERO

Ian Mackersey

RESCUE BELOW
ZERO

Published by Sapere Books.

20 Windermere Drive, Leeds, England, LS17 7UZ,
United Kingdom

saperebooks.com

ISBN: 978-1-80055-603-4.

TABLE OF CONTENTS

FOREWORD . . . 7
CHAPTER 1 . . . 9
CHAPTER 2 . . . 26
CHAPTER 3 . . . 38
CHAPTER 4 . . . 52
CHAPTER 5 . . . 72
CHAPTER 6 . . . 82
CHAPTER 7 . . . 92
CHAPTER 8 . . . 116
CHAPTER 9 . . . 138
CHAPTER 10 . . . 150
EPILOGUE . . . 163
ACKNOWLEDGEMENTS . . . 171
A NOTE TO THE READER . . . 172

FOREWORD

Between the mountains which stretch like a chain of Switzerlands along the east and west coasts of Greenland lies a huge, flat-topped sea of ice. Sixteen hundred miles long, 700 miles across at its widest and in parts 10,000 ft thick, it is the biggest relic of the Ice Age on earth today. Around its bleak edges sweep 100-mile-an-hour blizzards and in winter when a six months' cloak of darkness envelopes the far north it is gripped by temperatures of minus 90 degrees. Summer and winter between blizzards the most awesome feature of this big ice sheet is its great silence, a silence which deadens men's voices a few yards from their lips and gives them the feeling that in this numbing white void they are no longer part of the world they knew.

This is a story about the ice-cap, a recent and true story about eighteen men, thirty dogs and a big four-engined aircraft. It happened in September 1952. Six of the men were British explorers. Members of the British North Greenland Expedition, they were in the middle of the ice-cap, 8,000 ft above sea-level, 700 miles from the Pole by design. The others — seven Royal Air Force men, four British Army men and a United States Air Force officer — were dropping supplies to them. Their sudden arrival in a crash landing was unscheduled.

For nine days the crippled aircraft, the expedition's tiny tents, the men on the ice and the pilots of the U.S.A.F. whose resourcefulness finally averted a critical situation by two dramatic rescues, made world news.

But, as quickly as they had leapt onto the front pages the ice-cap men faded from the public eye. Within a few weeks they were back with their squadrons, and Army units. Today, eight months later, all that remains to mark their brief encounter with the expedition is a grey and red aircraft, slowly disappearing under the ever shifting Greenland snow.

CHAPTER 1

THE first Mike Clancy heard of the Greenland supply dropping business was from his signaller, Flight Sergeant Frank Burke. Burke had an uncanny facility for discovering everything that was "in the wind". He seemed to know about a special flight, who the crews were to be, which squadron was going, long before any of the others had an inkling of it.

"Know anything about Eskimos, Sir?" he asked.

"Not much," said Clancy.

"Well," said Burke with a grin, "you soon will. We're going to live among them. We're off to the North Pole."

Clancy said: "Look, I've just been sweating my way back from the Equator, my blood's thin. Don't talk about things like that; the thought of it makes me shiver."

That was in April, 1952. It was a crisp spring morning and Mike Clancy, a thirty-four-year-old flight commander of 47 Squadron was still in flying kit. Only ten minutes earlier he had trundled his big Transport Command Hastings aircraft onto the long concrete runway at Topcliffe in Yorkshire and taxied briskly across to the dispersals. It was the end of another trip. For the past five days he had been "staging" home from the Far East — flying a day — or a night — resting a day and so on, all the way from Singapore. The day before he had flown "U" for Uncle, his silver and grey Hastings, the military version of B.O.A.C.'s Hermes, a thousand miles from Malta to Lyneham in Wiltshire with a complement of sleepy-eyed troops — stretcher cases home from Korea. The troops had disembarked there, for Lyneham, perched on a Wiltshire hill, is the R.A.F.'s United Kingdom terminal. But for the aircraft that fly Transport Command's long-distance overseas routes it is not the end of the journey. In the greying hours before dawn Clancy and the six other members of his crew had climbed into the Hastings again to fly her back across England to their home station.

Now in the brightening daylight the crew jumped down from "Uncle" eager to make their respective reports, snatch a bite of breakfast, and hurry off to their families — or if they were single, to catch up on some lost sleep in the mess. It was when Mike Clancy strolled toward 47 Squadron's flight office that Burke broke the news about Greenland. Although he was Clancy's signaller he hadn't flown with him on this trip. Now his cheerful Lancashire face was leaning out of the flight office window bursting with information about supply dropping, Eskimos, the North Pole and Greenland.

Mike thought it was another leg-pull. As an Irishman serving in the R.A.F. he had grown used to that. He went into the flight office, climbed out of his overalls and set about all the paper work, the reports and documents that are the responsibility of Transport Command captains after every flight. Half an hour later he pushed the forms into the little wire basket, picked up his overnight bag, the bag he had lived out of for the last eleven days, the bag that had accompanied him on a round trip of 16,000 miles through Malta, Egypt, Iraq, Pakistan, Ceylon, Malaya and back again and set off for home. Then something crossed his mind. He went back to the phone.

"Get me the Flying Wing Adjutant"... "Hello, Dickie. Look, for O'Reilly's sake what's all this about the North Pole. Burke's been babbling something about Eskimos and Greenland."

Flight Lieutenant Richard Harben, A.F.C., Topcliffe's flying wing adjutant said, "Nice to hear the voice of Limerick again.

Yes, it's true. Transport Command Headquarters has asked us to supply aircraft and crews for a job in Greenland this summer. There's an expedition going there and we're going to supply them. The C.O. has called for volunteers. But don't worry, someone's already put your name down for you."

Cecilia was waiting at home for Mike. She had heard the Hastings circling before landing and his breakfast was in the pressure cooker. Home for the Clancys was a big 22-foot cream and green caravan in the woods 600 yards from the flight office. They lived there with their three sons, aged seven, three and two, along with a cluster of other R.A.F. caravanning families for whom — like the Clancys, these luxurious postwar homes on wheels have neatly solved the housing problem.

Three small demanding voices shot a torrent of questions: "What have you got for me Daddy?" "Did you remember my pineapple?" "Have you brought us any coconuts?" "How long are you staying?" "Good trip?" asked Cecilia. "How long have we got you for this time?"

"Average," said Mike. "But I'm off again — to the North Pole!"

Cecilia tried to hide her disappointment. She thought wistfully of the holiday they had planned, the holiday to Mike's homeland — Ireland. Like so many of their plans in the past it had to be abandoned. But as the wife of a Transport Command pilot she knew that it was the Service first: holidays often had to be taken quickly when opportunity offered.

That afternoon Mike Clancy learned more of the plans for what was to be one of the R.A.F.'s farthest north supply dropping operations. The squadron seethed with rumour. Some said they were bound for a highly secret base right on the North Pole itself, others that the Hastings were to be landed on the polar ice miles from any base, while a third and better informed school suggested that operations were to be conducted from a new American airfield somewhere inside the Arctic Circle.

There was intense friendly rivalry too. For 47 Squadron shared Topcliffe with another Hastings Squadron, No. 24 (Commonwealth) Squadron. Crews of both squadrons were eager that it should be their squadron chosen to go to Greenland. Both squadrons could boast fine records. 47 Squadron began in the days of "string-bag" fighters when bombs were hurled over the side by hand and pilots literally flew "by the seat of their pants". In 1949 it had been the first squadron in the Royal Air Force to be equipped with the Handley Page Hastings, a sleek, four-engined transport carrying fifty passengers and a crew of six. That same year at a colourful ceremony followed by a social evening at Hastings, the Sussex seaside town had formally "adopted" them.

24 Squadron was the Royal Air Force's V.I.P. transport squadron. One of its jobs in addition to long-distance route flying was to carry "very important people" wherever the needs of diplomacy or Government required them to go. Even older than 47 Squadron it was formed at Hounslow on September 1, 1915 as the R.F.C.s first single-seater fighter squadron. To preserve the Commonwealth spirit in the squadron its Commanding officers are selected in rotation from each of the Dominions. In the spring of 1952, a South African pilot, Major J. N. Robbs, D.F.C., was in command.

But there was no need for rivalry. Transport Command had decided that crews from both squadrons were to be represented in the operation. Group Captain J. A. C. Stratton, O.B.E., a wartime bomber pilot, Topcliffe's Station Commander, was to make the final selection.

Slowly a definite programme emerged from the uncertainty of rumour. For the first time Topcliffe learned what the Royal Air Force had been asked to do in the Arctic that summer.

The British North Greenland Expedition was going to Greenland for two years. Sponsored by the Scott Polar Research Institute, the Royal Geographical Society, the Royal Society and the three Services, it had three chief objectives: To raise the British flag again in the field of Arctic exploration; to give the Services experience in Arctic conditions and to test polar equipment; to undertake polar scientific research including investigation of the theory that Greenland is not a sub-continent but in fact a ring of coastal islands held together by a central 8,000-foot thick ice-cap. Base camp of the expedition was to be at Britannia Lake just north of the 77th Parallel in Queen Louise Land in north-east Greenland.

Not only was the expedition going to explore the 9,000-foot mountains in this region; it planned to cross the great inland ice and set up an ice-cap station, 300 miles inland from Britannia Lake where three men — to be relieved every five months — would keep a lonely vigil in a building under the snow, radioing back daily weather reports.

Biggest problem of all was that of supply. For the proposed base camp at Britannia Lake was effectively sealed off from the north-east Greenland coast by the twenty-mile wide bulk of the great Storstrømmen Glacier, an off-shoot of the ice-cap, which ran from north to south down the east side of the mountains of Queen Louise Land. Although it was planned to land the expedition's eight weasels — snow tractors — and trailer sledges on the coast by ship during the few brief weeks when the sea was ice-free, and drive them over the glacier to Britannia Lake, the surface of the Storstrømmen was too dangerously broken and crevassed to carry most of the expedition's 160 tons of food and equipment.

That was where the R.A.F. came in. Coastal Command Sunderlands were to airlift men, dogs and stores in to Britannia Lake from an ice-free sound on the coast 200 miles further south; later Transport Command Hastings were to drop supplies to the ice-cap station from a base on Greenland's west coast. In the summer of 1953 both Sunderlands and Hastings would fly further stores to the base camp and ice-cap station and the following year, in the summer of 1954, Coastal Command would help to bring the expedition home.

Twenty-five men were in the expedition — men of the Royal Navy, the Army, the Merchant Navy and civilian scientists. Among them were experienced glaciologists, geologists and meteorologists plus a Danish scientist representing the Danish Government.[1] The leader was a Naval officer, 41-year-old Commander Cortlandt J. W. Simpson, D.S.G., R.N. Two years earlier he had been an observer with a Danish expedition to Greenland. Flying in the expedition's aircraft along the north-east coast one day he had spotted a distant range of mountains with an unfrozen lake behind them. They were the 9,000-foot high peaks of then little-known Queen Louise Land. Few men had ever set foot among these forbidding-looking peaks and huge glaciers each big enough for all the glaciers of Switzerland to be packed with room to spare. It was the unfrozen lake that intrigued Commander Simpson. On its shores he saw great possibilities as a future base. So at his request he was put down on the nearby coast and, alone, made a five-day trek into the mountains to explore further the potentialities of what later

---

[1] In the winter of early 1953, the Danish member, Captain Jensen was tragically killed in Greenland. He fell while climbing with another member of the expedition in the mountains of Queen Louise Land.

was to be called Britannia Lake. From this solitary trek the British Expedition of 1952 began.

Despite its size — 840,000 square miles, next to Australia, the world's largest island — and its comparative proximity to northwest Europe and America, few people know much about Greenland. With the exception of the few avid readers of books on Arctic exploration and the early endurance sledge journeys across Greenland, the average citizen, if indeed he ever gives the place a thought, is probably content to accept the word of the hymn that it is a land of "icy mountains". Along Greenland's 3,000-mile coastline this is true enough — but the mountains represent only one-sixth of its total area. Most of the remainder — 700,000 square miles of it — is an almost flat ice ocean covering an area more than three times that of France.

The ice-cap is Greenland's most fascinating feature. Only occasionally visible from the coast as a smooth white lid, rather like the icing of an enormous Christmas cake, it fills the entire centre of the country between the mountains to a depth which is believed to range from 3,000 to 4,000 feet in the extreme south, to 10,000 feet and probably more in the north where Greenland is at its widest — 800 miles across. Through the ages the great hollow which the coastal mountains ring, filled up with the snowfalls of successive, almost thawless years, the tremendous weight of the mounting layers pressing and compressing the snow below until today the whole area between the mountains is packed with ice almost to the top of the surrounding peaks. It is only from the sea that Greenland's mountains appear in their true height. Inland, only the top few thousand feet poke above the ice that in the north is two miles deep. One of the British North Greenland Expedition's tasks was to try and calculate this depth with modern seismic equipment. For in places there is a theory that the great weight of billions of tons of ice has compressed the; earth's surface below into a huge U-shaped basin whose bottom may well be 12,000 or 13,000 feet below the top of the ice — and several thousand feet below sea level. If this were so, theoretically at least, a tunnel begun under the sea-bed off the Greenland coast and cut inland under the coastal mountains would eventually run into a wall of ice — the base of the ice-cap.

The ice-cap's only escape from the encircling mountains is in big glaciers in which it squeezes its way out to the coast through gaps in the peaks. In the narrow coastal fiords where the glaciers reach the sea their terminal faces are constantly breaking off. The process known as "calving" is the beginning of most of the icebergs which menace the shipping lanes of the North Atlantic. Hour after hour throughout the day the fiords reverberate to the crash of splitting ice as bergs — sometimes half a mile long and 300 feet high — plunge away from the glacier and float majestically out to sea and are carried south eventually to break up and melt in the warmer waters of the Atlantic's Gulf Stream. Nature works fast in Greenland. In some parts of the world glaciers move a ponderous few inches a week. Here in places the great ice chunks are disgorged at the rate of 60 feet a day.

It is among this pattern of tall jagged mountains, deep fiords and crashing ice that Greenland's 18,000 inhabitants live. They are mostly of Eskimo and Danish origin — for Greenland is a proud possession of Denmark. It has had associations with Scandinavia dating back to the tenth century. It was at the end of this century that the Icelander, Eric the Red, established a small Norse colony in Greenland which flourished for 500 years before it was abandoned in the fifteenth century. Many famous explorers subsequently "discovered" the country but throughout, the Dano-Norwegian kings, who also reigned over the Faroe Islands and Iceland, continued to make it clear that they also had sovereignty over Greenland, even though for several hundred years they had little direct link with the big island. When in 1814, the Napoleonic wars separated Denmark and Norway, Greenland stayed with Denmark. Since then Danish sovereignty over the whole territory has been universally recognized — with one exception. Between the First and Second World Wars Norway began to occupy some uninhabited strips of the coast, but the International Court of Justice declared this illegal. The Norwegians withdrew.

The narrow habitable strips of the Greenland coast between the mountains and the sea today represent a curious blend of the modern and the primitive. At the little townships — the biggest boasting a population of only 1200 — modern buildings, power stations, shops with neatly overalled assistants, printing works, hospitals, a radio station — even a "Parliament" or representative National Council as it is known, which meets at Gothab, the west coast capital, stand side by side with stone and turf houses, the kyak, seal oil lamps and sealskin clothes which many Eskimos still wear. There are few roads and all communication is by sea. In fact the sea and its harvest is the basis of Greenland's economy. The hunting of sea animals and fishing is virtually the only industry. The mountains contain copper, gold, silver, nickel and iron but most mining efforts have been beaten by the harsh climate — the coast is under heavy snow from early autumn until late spring — the winter darkness, the difficulties of hewing the solid mountain rock and the long sea voyages to overseas markets.

But today Greenland is assuming a new significance, a previously undreamt of one. The development of the long-range aircraft and the tension between Russia and her satellites and the Western World have made this big blizzard-swept island a centre of vital strategic importance. North Greenland lies in the middle of the great circle air route between North America and Russia. The advantage of air bases there is obvious and America has not been slow to make use of this. Under defence agreements signed in 1941 and ten years later in 1951, the United States Air Force has established several bases there. Best known are the "Bluie" chain of aerodromes — Bluie West 1 at the head of a bleak fiord at the southern tip of Greenland, Bluie West 8, 450 miles further north on the west coast deep inside 100-mile long Sondrestrom Fiord and Bluie East 2 near Angmagssalik, 450 miles north of Bluie West 1 on the east coast. They were staging posts during the war for short-range aircraft being ferried across the Atlantic.

Greenland has a further importance in the modern flying era; it is a breeding ground of much of the weather subsequently felt in the North Atlantic and North-West Europe. Reporting stations there are essential if the weather forecaster is to get anything like a true picture of conditions to come. In the last war the Germans realized this, and in the first two years of hostilities they made several attempts to establish fortified weather stations on the east coast. But each expedition was captured before it ever set foot ashore. In August, 1942, however, a more determined attempt succeeded — at least temporarily. Under command of a Lieutenant Ritter, a German party landed on Sabine Island in North-east Greenland and set up a meteorological station whose object was to radio advanced weather reports to the Luftwaffe, to North Atlantic

U-boats and to German blockade runners. Aircraft from Norway helped to supply the Nazis in their precarious outpost.

During the winter of 1942 the Germans decided to improve their radio forecasting facilities and seized the Allied radio station at nearby Eskimoness. This was their undoing. The Americans decided that it was time they got rid of the enemy in their midst. As soon as the Arctic night had faded sufficiently in the spring of 1943, American Liberators flew to Sabine Island and destroyed the German buildings including a 200-ton enemy trawler frozen into the ice off the island. Even this set-back failed to deter the German High Command. Throughout 1944 fresh attempts were made to re-establish posts on the east coast but none succeeded. American coastguard cutters sank one German trawler, captured another caught in the ice and found a third abandoned. A freshly established weather station on the east coast was destroyed despite the efforts of a Luftwaffe bomber to intervene.

In 1951 rumours began to reach England of a huge base which the Americans were said to be building in north Greenland. Guarded reports spoke of a mammoth secret construction programme employing fleets of ships and thousands of workmen to lay down a great strategic bomber base; Operation Blue Jay it was called. Not until eighteen months later in mid-1952 was the security lid lifted and the United States Defence Department made public details of a big base nearing completion at Thule on the north-west Greenland coast, 900 miles only from the Pole.

At the beginning of 1951 Thule, a barren, windswept valley, rock-strewn and treeless comprised a primitive Eskimo village, a tiny crushed rock landing ground and an isolated joint American-Danish weather station manned by eighteen observers. Within a few months a gigantic task force of 8,500 men arrived. With them by sea and air came trucks, bulldozers, huge mechanical shovels and all the paraphernalia of a major base. And within eighteen months America's biggest secret military operation since the Normandy invasion had transformed the valley into one of the world's major air bases — a strategically priceless outpost standing guardian midway between North America and Russia — 2,400 miles from New York, 2,780 miles from Moscow.

At R.A.F. Topcliffe in April 1952 much of the conversation was of Greenland. Pilots and navigators eagerly devoured all the scant information they could find about the mysterious icy continent, signallers made discreet investigations of their own into the existence of radio stations in the area, the flight engineers' "union" held its own unofficial discussion into the problems of the operation of aircraft engines in Arctic conditions and the air quartermasters — the R.A.F.'s flight stewards — pondered on the all-important business of feeding hungry crews with appetites whetted by high latitudes.

Meanwhile 47 and 24 Squadrons went about the routine of busy Transport Command squadrons. Hastings aircraft roared in and out on schedules to the Canal Zone, Rhodesia, Singapore, and Germany. And tension in Egypt demanded a constant nucleus of aircraft and crews on permanent standby in case a sudden trooping operation was necessary in the Middle East. Then one day in April a list of crews for a special operation was posted in both squadrons. It was Greenland.

Two Hastings were to go. Mike Clancy was to be captain of one and twenty-seven-year-old Flight Lieutenant David Wright, a post-war trained R.A.F. pilot already with 1400 hours in his log-book, the other. Average age of the crews was thirty.

Mike Clancy, a stocky blue-eyed Irishman with a rich brogue and his roots deep in the old soil of Limerick had been in the R.A.F. sixteen years. Descended of a long line of professional soldiers who through the centuries fought in every war that threatened the fervent independence of the "soil" he describes himself as an Irish mercenary who "spent my schooldays, bedad, dreaming chiefly of travel and flying". In 1936 when he joined the R.A.F. as an equipment assistant he was to get a full share of both. The R.A.F. sent him to Habbanyia in the Iraq desert near Bagdad and there he got his first taste of flying — as a part time air gunner in Valencias, a lumbering old biplane. In May, 1941, war came to the peaceful desert airfield. Italian bombers roared over excitedly sprinkling Habbanyia with bombs. Corporal Clancy found himself suddenly in a ditch with a splinter wound that prevented him from sitting down for several months. Lying in that dusty ditch calling the wrath of St Patrick down on the spalpeens of Italian pilots overhead he had decided that his Irish pride could only be vindicated in one way. To get on equal terms with the enemy he would have to become a pilot. He did.

Eighteen months later when he went home to Limerick on leave he wore pilot's wings and the thin blue braid of a Pilot Officer. He had decided by now that he was best cut out for night-fighters — but the R.A.F. thought otherwise. He was sent to Pershore to train on Wellington bombers but there he was seriously injured in a crash when one of his engines failed and it was late 1944 before he had recovered sufficiently to be allowed to fly again. By the time he had been converted onto Lancasters the war was over. Transport Command, however, was in need of pilots so Mike applied to join. But the Transport selection board were sceptical of the mercenary from Limerick. He didn't have enough experience on heavy multi-engined aircraft, they said. Mike had to do some fast talking but in the end his keenness won the day. He was sent to a Dakota conversion school and in 1946 joined 31 Squadron in Batavia evacuating Japanese prisoners from camps in Java and Sumatra. After that he was posted to another Dakota squadron in Singapore, route-flying and supply-dropping to troops on antiterrorist operations in the Malayan jungle.

One day in 1949 when the Berlin airlift was at its height and aircraft of all shapes and sizes were streaming up and down the corridors to and from the German capital an R.A.F. Dakota landed at Gatow with a load of young British soldiers. The troops had disembarked and were standing chattering in a group beside the aircraft discussing what for most of them had been their first flight. Soon the navigator, signaller and co-pilot climbed out. The soldiers heard one of them say: "What about the skipper. We'd better help him out." While the curious troops watched, the crew went back into the Dakota and emerged supporting surely the great-grandfather of all pilots. Bent with age he supported his groaning frame with a stick; the wings on his crumpled flying overalls were almost obscured by a flowing white beard and from the dark glasses he wore it looked as if he was either blind or very nearly so. As the crew solicitously helped this decrepit figure down the aircraft's steps he cursed them freely and laid about them with his stick.

"Make way for the captain", the crew shouted. With incredulous stares the soldiers moved aside and the grunting, complaining figure feeling his way with his stick, stumped across the tarmac and disappeared into one of the buildings. Among the group beside the aircraft a voice tinged with awe said: "Christ did *he* fly us here? Looks more like Rip Van Winkle than a pilot to me." Over at flying control people were staring at four R.A.F. men who were roaring with laughter.

One of them held a false beard and a pair of sun-glasses in his hand. His name was Clancy.

Since the Berlin airlift on which he flew many sorties Mike Clancy had flown 600,000 miles — flying first Yorks and later Hastings on Transport Command's overseas trunk routes. In the spring of 1952 his total flying hours were approaching the 3,000 mark.

Clancy's co-captain was twenty-eight-year-old Flight Lieutenant Ted Adair. Placid and soft-spoken he was a Londoner, had been a glider-pilot at the Rhine crossing during the war and now he and his wife were caravan neighbours of the Clancys.

Senior navigator was Flight Lieutenant Reg Michie. He was short, stocky, twenty-eight and had a reputation as the squadron wit. He was to share the navigation and all the special problems it involves in high latitudes where the magnetic compass often points anywhere but north, with Flying Officer Les Richardson a cheerful post-war trained navigator of twenty-six.

For his Signaller — the R.A.F.'s post-war name for wireless operator — Clancy had Burke. A thirty-three-year-old Lancashireman from Rochdale, Frank Burke was 47 Squadron's "family man"; he was married with four children. He had flown many wartime operations with Bomber Command. Switched to Transport Command after the war he was one of Topcliffe's fastest men on the Morse key, a reputation which had earned him the nickname "Electric Fingers". The flight engineer was another N.C.O. — Master Engineer Richard Mosley. Thirty-four, he came from Darlington and had been a flight engineer instructor. The four 1,675 h.p. piston Hercules engines which power the Hastings were his special responsibility. And finally there was the Air

Quartermaster, thirty-four-year-old Flight Sergeant Boyd. Better known to the crew as "Chiefy" he had been in the R.A.F. longer than any of the others. He signed on back in 1935 in a ground trade. But Boyd was not happy with service on the ground. Determined to fly in any capacity he became an air quartermaster. With Transport Command his appetite for flying was well satisfied; he was in the air for as much as 100 hours a month.

Flight Lieutenant Wright's co-captain was Flying Officer Ian Iddison. Post-war trained he was twenty-seven and married. He had a Service name as a boxer of some skill. Navigators were Flight Lieutenant Brian Adlington and Sergeant R. A. Barnes; signaller, Sergeant R. E. Bowler: flight-engineer, Master Engineer E.R. Mears; and air quartermaster, Flight Sergeant J. Fairburn.

Meanwhile in London plans for the British North Greenland Expedition were rapidly shaping. At expedition headquarters, a room in the Admiralty's Queen Anne's Mansions, Whitehall, with the walls decorated with Arctic photographs and maps there were frequent conferences of representatives of the three services. The Army, too, had a part to play. It was keen to learn more about Arctic supply dropping, an operation of which it had almost no experience. Its Air Transport Training and Development Centre at Old Sarum in Wiltshire was to provide despatches to fly in the Hastings and heave the supplies out over the ice-cap; it was also responsible for crating and packing the air drop supplies — eighty-two tons in all — for shipment to Thule by cargo ship. An R.A.S.C. officer was to command the Army detachment.

In April, three months before the expedition was due to land in north-east Greenland — some by R.A.F. flying-boat, others and the bulk of the stores by a small Norwegian motor ship the

Tottan — Mike Clancy was asked to report to R.A.F. Lyneham. He was to meet Commander Simpson and fly with him to Paris. There members of *Expeditions Polaires Françaises* who had recently returned from a lonely two years' vigil at an ice station in the middle of Greenland were to tell them all they knew of ice-cap supply dropping. The expedition which had been led by M. Paul Emile Victor had been supplied by chartered Skymasters from Iceland.

CHAPTER 2

MIKE CLANCY had heard a lot about Commander Simpson. In the past weeks the Commander had become something of a legendary figure at Topcliffe. Mike said: "I was expecting to meet a big burly character or someone looking like the popular pictures of Scott of the Antarctic complete with beard". Instead he was introduced in the sunshine at Lyneham that morning to a short, slightly-built man in a civilian suit. The man had a duffle-coat slung over his arm. To Mike he looked more like a country parson than the leader of one of Britain's biggest Arctic expeditions. But there were features about this man of the sea which commanded attention. Most striking were his piercing blue eyes which seemed, so Mike thought, to be swiftly sizing Him up. But, after all, the ice-cap men were going to be very dependent on the R.A.F. pilots and the vital stores they were to drop.

Commander Simpson's passion for polar exploration was a development of his interest in mountaineering, a recreation he took up in 1938 when he was twenty-nine. When he went to Dartmouth at thirteen he was continuing a long association his family has had with the sea. His father was a Rear Admiral, his grandfather, a Vice-Admiral. His mother was Australian, the daughter of a big sheep-station owning family. Early in the last war Commander Simpson became an anti-submarine specialist and shortly after was in H.M.S. *Medway* when she was torpedoed and sank within fifteen minutes in the Mediterranean. In 1943 he joined the 16th Destroyer Flotilla on anti E-boat duties off England's east coast and for one night action earned a D.S.C. Promoted Commander in 1948 his thoughts turned to polar exploration. He decided to sound the Admiralty on the possibility and prepared a plan for a small naval expedition to explore the little-known interior of Scoresby Sound, a huge fiord system on Greenland's east coast at the 70th Parallel. The plan was turned down. The Navy hadn't the resources at that time, he was told, but for Commander Simpson there was a ray of hope — he was asked to keep his plan alive for possible future use. Meanwhile the opportunity of polar exploration came to him from another direction. In 1950 a Danish expedition went to north-east Greenland; the Admiralty said he could go as an observer. During that summer of 1950 in Greenland Commander Simpson became more convinced than ever that a British expedition should be given an opportunity there. Back in London he put his plans forward again. And to his delight the Admiralty now said yes. But before a full-scale expedition could be landed on the far from hospitable ice-strewn Greenland coast it was decided to have a closer look at the territory.

Early in the summer of 1951 a Coastal Command Sunderland from Pembroke Dock in Wales flew Commander Simpson and four other members of the expedition-to-be to north-east Greenland for a six weeks' reconnaissance. The plan was that the Sunderland should fly via Reykjavik and Ella Island, a Danish outpost on the 73rd Parallel to Seal Lake, a long narrow mountain-locked strip of water 700 miles from the Pole at Latitude 77° N. Commander Simpson and his men were to be put ashore in R.A.F. dinghies at the western end of the lake near the tongue of the great Storstrømmen Glacier. The aircraft was then to fly to the eastern end and pick up a Danish trapper and six huskies, flying them back to join Commander Simpson's party. The pilot, Wing Commander G.

G. N. Barret, A.F.C. and Bar, was not altogether pleased at the prospect of flying a load of ferocious huskies but Commander Simpson assured him that the dogs would merely "howl and stink".

The whole success of the operation depended on the water both at Ella Island and Seal Lake being sufficiently free of ice to land the Sunderland. It was very much a pioneer flight for Seal Lake was completely uncharted and no aircraft had ever landed there before. Wing Commander Barrett prayed that the lake would be deep enough to take his flying-boat yet not too deep to anchor it. Of the existence of underwater obstacles neither he nor anyone else had the least clue.

The Sunderland flew to Reykjavik on July 23. There they met M. Victor whom they found "extremely knowledgeable on things both arctic and antarctic" — at that time *Expeditions Polaires Françaises* had one expedition on the Greenland icecap, another in the Antarctic. When the Sunderland flew up to Ella Island two days later M. Victor went with them. Glorious weather favoured the flight and four hours from Reykjavik the flying-boat alighted between icebergs and big pieces of floating ice beside the barren rock mass of Ella Island. Wing Commander Barrett carefully taxied through the ice to anchor in fifteen fathoms beside the wooden huts of the Danish survey party who were charting east Greenland using three Cansos — amphibious Catalinas. The Danes were immediately hospitable; their leader Colonel Helk invited the party ashore to a musk-ox roast. This was no small honour for the Greenland musk-ox is dying out and the number that may be taken in a season is strictly limited. The Danes had shot this one the previous day specially for the Sunderland men. It made a delicious feast and the hosts spoke excellent English. Later the R.A.F. reciprocated with a cocktail party aboard the

Sunderland. Crew and passengers slept aboard that night although the sun did not set.

On July 28 the Sunderland flew on up the Greenland coast to see if it was possible to land at Seal Lake. Colonel Helk had been pessimistic about their chances and when the eastern end of the desolate thirty-mile strip of water showed up among the surrounding mountains — at this time of year snow-free — his pessimism seemed justified — the lake was covered in ice. The only exception was a small muddy puddle at the very end, "no bigger than Piccadilly Circus". Four miles south of the lake down a river they found the trapper's hut. As the Sunderland roared low over his lonely little home the man came out and waved reassuringly. As it was not possible to pick him and his huskies up Wing Commander Barrett climbed up to 3,000 feet and cruised back down the lake to have a look at the western end. For twenty-six miles the lake was frozen over and the hearts of Commander Simpson and his four men sank. It looked as if the long flight had been in vain. Then suddenly round a bend of the lake the last four miles showed up — apart from a few isolated chunks of ice it was clear.

Wing Commander Barrett brought the big flying-boat round in a long low sweep over the muddy brown water. After dropping a flame float to check the wind direction he made six low runs into wind while everybody peered anxiously down, each trying privately to make his own assessment of the depth. But the Wing Commander was satisfied that it was safe. He told Commander Simpson he was prepared to land.

But before landing there was another job to be done. At the western end of Seal Lake was a big glacier — Lion Glacier — twenty miles beyond which in the mountains of Queen Louise Land there were several smaller lakes nearer the ice-cap which the expedition later planned to cross. After they had been landed at Seal Lake Commander Simpson and his party were now going to link up with the trapper whose dogs they wanted to use to sledge across the Lion Glacier and look for a good site for the expedition's base camp, a site which they hoped would be beside a lake on which flying-boats could later land them and their supplies. This was the uncharted country into which Commander Simpson had peeped the year before.

Now to save the Commander and his party dragging all their stores across the Lion Glacier the Sunderland was to parachute a month's supplies beside a likely lake. So they flew across the glacier and circled the mountainous approaches of Queen Louise Land. After a consultation with M. Victor who had become almost as enthusiastic about the forthcoming British expedition as he was for his own big polar organization, Commander Simpson chose a likely dropping zone on a hill beside a lake. One by one the supplies went floating down all landing nicely within a hundred-yard circle.

Back at Seal Lake Wing Commander Barrett dropped a smoke path of three more flame floats and put the Sunderland down in a nice landing — just 700 miles from the Pole. The aircraft anchored easily sixty yards from the southern shore, this time in only three fathoms. The Wing Commander wrote later: "Our only difficulty in anchoring was the annoying presence of small icebergs. Several excursions were made ashore in a J-type dinghy and a large hot lunch was prepared for the explorers before they were mercilessly cast off on the glacier. As it was out of the question to collect the trapper and dogs from the other end of the lake, Commander Simpson decided to meet them on foot — a day's travel — and we undertook to drop the trapper a message. At 15.30 we saw the party ashore with our good wishes and took off from Seal Lake fifteen minutes later happy in the knowledge that our main job had been successfully accomplished. Approaching the eastern end of the lake at 3,000 feet I noticed something flashing in my eye: it was the trapper's heliograph — a most efficient method of signalling. He had gathered his rucksack, dogs and sandwiches and had tramped the four miles to the end of the lake, obviously expecting us to land on the tiny ice-free puddle. But he was quick to understand we had no such intentions, and that a message was to be dropped. We saw him retrieve it and he waved to acknowledge the, for him, disappointing contents."

The Sunderland flew back to Pembroke Dock and a month later returned to Seal Lake to pick up Commander Simpson and his men. At Reykjavik where bad weather had delayed him Wing Commander Barrett met Colonel Helk who was returning to Denmark. The colonel was worried about Commander Simpson's party having failed to make radio contact with them. He also brought the disquieting news that winter ice — it was only August 27 — was already beginning to form on some of the northern lakes. If the flying-boat was to beat the approaching ice and collect the reconnaissance party before the Arctic winter set in there was no time to lose.

The morning of August 28 brought no improvement in the spell of bad weather. But the midday report from Scoresby Sound, south of Ellis Island gave a 1,500 foot cloud base and twenty miles visibility. Wing Commander Barrett decided to take off. At the 66th Parallel off the north-west tip of Iceland the Sunderland ran into cloud and rain. While flying through it on instruments, radio contact was made with two of the Danish Cansos going in the opposite direction. The Danes told them they would break through the weather at the 68th Parallel. And they were right. Shortly after the cloud base rose to 3,000 feet and visibility increased to sixty miles.

At Ella Island there was further disturbing news. The Danes there had just had a radio message from Danmarkshavn weather station, thirty miles east of Seal Lake to say that Commander Simpson's dogs had been found running wild, hungry and in poor condition at the *eastern* end of the lake. Added to the Danish Colonel's misgivings this information almost seemed to confirm that the party was in trouble. The brief three-hour Arctic night was all too long for Wing Commander Barrett that night. At first light he left for Seal Lake.

A wave of relief went through everybody aboard the Sunderland when the lake appeared below — ice-free. The trapper's hut was empty and at the western end of the lake where the five men had landed a month before, the tent, sleds and yellow R.A.F. dinghy showed up against the grey shingle — but no sign of life. The Wing Commander landed and went ashore to investigate. The tent had obviously not been opened for several weeks; the knot was weathered tight. Inside were various pieces of equipment, food and clothing; outside two odd boots, a tripod, and other odds and ends — but not a clue to the whereabouts of the five explorers. The R.A.F. men were mystified.

Then one of the Sunderland crew, Flight Lieutenant Morrison, spotted footprints in the shingle. How recent they were it was hard to say but they followed them for 200 yards toward the glacier at the lake's end. Suddenly someone shouted: "Look, over at the foot of the glacier, there's somebody coming". A mile away Commander Simpson was hurrying back to the tent. Behind him came four more specks. As the five sunburned, bearded figures approached the R.A.F. men yelled with relief — even those still aboard the aircraft out in the lake joined in — now that their big anxiety had been dispelled.

Commander Simpson soon explained the mystery of the dogs. A month earlier when they had set out on their glacier journey they had decided that the ice was too rough for the huskies and sleds. So they had shot a bull musk-ox and left it by the tent, adequate food for more than a month they thought. But they hadn't reckoned with the voracious appetite of the six perpetually hungry huskies. With no thought for the future the dogs had gorged themselves on the ox, quickly picking it clean. They then turned their attention to the tent which they ransacked, after which they cleared off, roaming thirty miles to the far end of the lake in search of more food.

Meanwhile over in Queen Louise Land Commander Simpson's party had found a lake which they considered suitable for a Sunderland. Hopefully they called it Adastra Lake. Five miles long by two miles wide it lay between the Lion Glacier on the east and the Unicorn Glacier on the west. Its big, white-splayed tongue running down to the lake edge, the Unicorn Glacier was to Commander Simpson, a highway of some potential. In a long majestic sweep it led onto the big ice plateau. It was the gateway to the ice-cap.

Although his rendezvous for August 25 had been fixed at Seal Lake Commander Simpson waited at Adastra Lake until the 27th. He hoped that when the Sunderland returned and found they had not arrived back at Seal Lake it would fly over Queen Louise Land, spot them and attempt a landing on the lake. But when the aircraft had not shown up on the 27th shortage of food compelled a retreat. And so it happened that the coincidence of the Sunderland's late arrival and the party's food crisis brought both to Seal Lake within an hour of each other — four days after rendezvous day. Two days later Commander Simpson was back in London.

Within half an hour of meeting Commander Simpson at Lyneham that April morning, Mike Clancy knew more about Greenland than most of his colleagues in the R.A.F. To Mike, the Commander "seemed to radiate a power of energy. He was wholly and utterly absorbed in the big task ahead and his enthusiasm for the expedition and Greenland was somehow transmitted to me. I quickly found that he expected the same enthusiasm from all those associated with him in this icy enterprise".

Clancy and Commander Simpson flew from Lyneham to Paris in an R.A.F. Anson. With them went Squadron Leader B. V. Hunter, D.F.C., — his job was liaison between Transport Command and the Expedition — and an Army major, a supply dropping expert. During the ninety-minute flight Clancy absorbed himself in a report of Simpson's on Greenland. In it there were photographs — the first Clancy had ever seen of Greenland — of great mountain ranges, enormous glaciers and barren coastal hills flanked by thick ice. When the Anson dropped in past the Eiffel Tower and landed at Villacoublay on the southern outskirts of Paris Mike felt as enthusiastic about Greenland as Commander Simpson.

A British Embassy major met them at the airport and they were quickly whisked by car through the spring blossom of outer Paris into the bedlam of the Champs Elysees to the headquarters of *Expeditions Polaires Françaises*. M. Victor himself was away in America but one of his pilots, a stocky ruddy-complexioned Frenchman and several other members of the organization were able to answer most of Simpson's, Clancy's and Hunter's questions about ice-cap supply dropping.

The conference was held in a remarkable room bristling with the spirit of the Arctic. The walls were covered with Polar maps and photographs and on a table was a big clay model of Greenland with a scale replica of M. Victor's ice-cap station complete with model wind generators, exhaust pipes and radio masts poking out of the snow. One photograph was of special interest to the Englishmen. It showed a big weasel train on the Greenland ice flying the French pennants. Beside it was a group of goggled, bearded men. Commander Simpson said: "I'm afraid our expedition will be much smaller than this. We will be walking in to our ice-cap station and our few weasels will follow later."

During the conference Simpson, Clancy and Hunter plied the French with questions. A pretty auburn-haired French girl made furious shorthand notes of it all and interpreted where necessary — but Commander Simpson had a good knowledge of French. Clancy asked them if the aircraft had had much difficulty in locating the camp on the ice-cap — a tiny speck in a huge featureless sea of ice. What sort of radio aids had they used? From what height did they drop the supplies? How did the pilots judge their height above the snow?

The French were profusely polite and endlessly patient. They said they had homed the supply aircraft to their camp with both medium frequency direction finding radio which the aircraft could pick up 250 miles away and with a Eureka radar beacon which had a smaller range — about eighty miles. The Skymaster pilots had had little difficulty judging the run in — they used the huts and equipment on the ground to assess their height. To save the expense of parachutes they had free-dropped as much of the supplies as possible straight out of the aircraft through a specially built despatching chute onto the snow. From what height? About ten metres, the French said casually.

Mike Clancy raised his Irish eyebrows at this, and Squadron Leader Hunter said "My God — thirty feet." Mike's thoughts flashed to the Hastings with its 112-foot wingspan. Running in at 120 knots with the ground — if you could judge it accurately which was unlikely anyway — only a fifth of a wingspan's distance below didn't allow for much error of judgment. He thought of drops he had made in Dakotas in Malaya and Java over jungle and paddy fields from eighty feet and heavens knew how close the ground looked then.

But the French didn't seem to think there was anything very exceptional about ten metres. With a wave of his arms the ruddy-cheeked pilot said: "We used the talk-down; it was easy." Talk-down, he explained had been conducted by the men on the snow by radio to the pilot. As the aircraft approached, the men on the ground would call through the radio "Up a little, down a little, hold it there" and so on, positioning the pilot at what they could judge as the vital ten metres. For it appeared that above this height the supplies scattered too far from the camp and dug themselves too deeply in the snow. It was either from ten metres or from a much safer height with parachutes — but then parachutes raised costs.

After lunch in a Parisian cafe at which the English officers were feted with a very special brand of pink wine they were taken to a cinema which was screening the film of M. Victor's ice-cap expedition. It was an absorbing film and sequences shot from over a Skymaster pilot's shoulder showed Clancy all too vividly how a small collection of huts on the snow looks to a pilot flashing by only thirty feet up. When the Anson flew them back to Lyneham that evening instead of the blue

Channel below him Mike saw a shimmering white stretch of snow — and the tiny specks of a little French camp.

CHAPTER 3

A HUNDRED feet above a big Wiltshire field eight miles from Boscombe Down a Hastings swept in at 120 knots. A cluster of various shaped bundles showered down from its rear door and bounced along the ground. Some of them burst open. Nearby a bushy-moustached major with a merry twinkle in his eyes stood beside a portable radio set. He had a notebook in his hand. The receiver was crackling with a voice whose Irish brogue even the radio's distortion could not completely destroy. "Baker Mike to D.Z. How was that one now?" it was asking. The major whose name was Barker-Simson and who wore the flashes of the R.A.S.C. picked up his microphone. "D.Z. to Baker Mike" he said crisply, "that drop was quite nice. Some of the packets burst but they won't do that on the snow."

It was May 27. In the Hastings were Mike Clancy and David Wright. They had been sent to Boscombe, headquarters of the Ministry of Supply's secret Aeroplane and Armament Experimental Establishment to make dropping tests, and to discover the ideal height from which to "free-drop" the expedition's stores without the expense of parachutes. They were practising on the A and A.E.E.s experimental dropping zone.

Major Barker-Simson came from the Army Air Transport Training and Development Centre at nearby Old Sarum. He was to lead the team of Army despatchers who were going to Greenland with the two Hastings and now he had positioned himself beside the D.Z. to watch dummy stores pushed out from various heights. The day before the Hastings had experimented with a roller conveyor along which the loads could be trundled toward the door and then pushed out. It was designed to speed up dropping and to relieve the despatches of some of the burden of lumping heavy crates about the fuselage. But the wooden battens on the crates jammed between the rollers and the conveyor was abandoned in favour of a platform placed beside the open door. The supplies were loaded onto the platform and tipped off it over the dropping zone.

As each load came down Major Barker-Simson noted the result and an Army photographer took pictures. Flying upwind with 30 degrees of flap lowered to knock his airspeed back to between 115 and 120 knots Clancy flew up the field fist at 100 feet, then at 80 feet and finally at 50 feet. The French had advocated 30 feet but at Boscombe that morning 50 feet proved to be quite low enough.

Barker-Simson was specially interested to see just how far the loads were spread by the wind and their initial forward momentum on their brief journey down. Eight thousand feet up on the ice-cap a man's breath comes slower than at sea level and the expedition didn't want to spend any more time than was necessary scouring the snow for far-flung packages. The trials showed that from 100 feet the sacks, barrels and crates were scattered over 800 yards of the field; from 80 feet over 500-600 yards. But at 50 feet the "spread" was a comfortable 200 yards.

Four types of container were tested — wooden boxes, cylindrical cardboard cartons, plywood cylinders and jute sacks stuffed with wood shavings. On landing the boxes disintegrated, smashing the tins inside, the carton ends burst open shooting the contents violently onto the ground, the plywood cylinder walls were crushed and the stores scattered for yards around. Only the sack loads came through with flying colours. Apart from a few bent tins their contents were undamaged. Admittedly many of the crates were shattered on the hard grass surface whereas on the ice-cap the impact would be cushioned by the snow. Nevertheless it was decided to use the sacks where possible and to push them out from 50 feet.

Radio trials followed. Finding a couple of tiny tents in the middle of the Greenland ice was going to be rather like looking for a floating bottle reported at a certain position in the Channel. True, the ice camp's exact latitude and longitude would be known but there are no aids to navigation on the cap and the best a navigator could hope for was to get his pilot as near as possible to the specks on the snow by dead reckoning. After that the Hastings were going to depend on radio homing from the men on the ground. The ice-cap party was to be equipped with two Army radios one for long-range work and the other for talking to the aircraft when they were within five to ten miles range. It was also to have a Eureka radar beacon whose waves were to be picked up on the Hastings' Rebecca screens and the aircraft led — it was hoped — straight to the camp regardless of the visibility.

Clancy and Wright practised with identical equipment at Topcliffe. For hours they flew round Yorkshire calling the Army radios back at the airfield from all directions and from increasing distances until reception faded out. The radios worked well — at least in Yorkshire they did.

After free-dropping trials with jerrycans at Watchfield and an air support course at Abingdon the two pilots started low flying practice to gain confidence in handling the Hastings at the levels at which they would have to operate over the ice-cap. They flew down the runway at Topcliffe at 50 feet and later went out over the sea off Scarborough. Taking it in turns at the controls they used the radio altimeter to creep down to and maintain precisely 50 feet. While one of them flew the other would sit beside him with his eyes glued to the radio altimeter chanting the decreasing heights in twenty-foot stages. It was a delicate and exacting business. Fishermen off the Yorkshire coast were startled time and time again during the training programme by the big silver and white aircraft which burst suddenly on them out of the sea haze clearing their masts by, the trawlermen swore, mere "flickering inches!"

Before the British North Greenland Expedition sailed, a proving flight was made in June to the new United States air base at Thule from which the Hastings were to fly their supply dropping sorties to the ice-cap station — 480 miles inland. Commander Simpson also wanted to meet the American commander there to make arrangements for handling his stores which were due to arrive by sea as soon as the winter pack-ice cleared sufficiently to allow ships in to Thule's newly-built port. One crew was selected for the flight from the two already chosen. Mike Clancy was to be captain, David Wright co-pilot, Flight Lieutenants Michie and Adlington, navigators, Flight Sergeant Burke, signaller, plus Master Engineer Mosley and "Chiefy" Boyd as air quartermaster.

The Hastings for the flight was specially modified for cold weather flying. In view of the severe icing risks in Greenland the aircraft's de-icing system was enlarged. Ice is one of the pilots biggest enemies. It can gather anywhere from the leading edges of the wing and tail plane to the blades of propellers even though they may be spinning too fast to be seen. Its build-up is often sudden and swift; in fact big aircraft have been forced down and crashed when ice accretion has so distorted the streamlining of the wings that they have lost all power of lift and the aircraft has stalled. In the Hastings ice is counteracted by anti-icing fluid which is pumped, when ice threatens, onto all leading edges of the flying surfaces including the propeller blades. And so that the pilot's view is not obstructed by ice the co-pilot has a hand control by which he can spray fluid over the outside of the windscreen.

The Hastings for the proving flight had bigger de-icing fluid tanks fitted, the oil dilution system was wired up so that petrol could be added to the engine oil to make starting easier in the Arctic cold, the engine boost control restrictors were removed to give the pilot a quick build up of power when he needed it, special mats were fitted inside to safeguard against slipping on the floor should it become icy, cold weather covers were loaded aboard with which to protect the undercarriage should it be parked in snow, extra radio crystals were added to cope with the American frequencies, and finally the Hastings had its wing tips, fin and rudder painted red — an aid to search recognition in the event of a forced landing in the snow.

Clancy and Wright then began radio-range flying practice and reacquainted themselves with the technique of I.L.S. — Instrument Landing System — both favourites of the United States Air Force. They took a Hastings to Bristol and Prestwick in Scotland to practice on the ranges there. Then they took their crew to Shawbury in Shropshire for a special arctic briefing.

On June 4 they flew to Lyneham, picked up Commander Simpson and two Transport Command officers and set off for Thule. It was a thirteen-hour flight with one stop at Keflavik, Iceland's bleak trans-Atlantic airfield, thirty miles from Reykjavik. From Iceland to Thule Mike flew at 11,000 feet above cloud. As they approached the Greenland coast everybody craned their necks for a glimpse of the famous ice-cap but were disappointed. The whole of southern Greenland was heavily veiled in cloud, and although they flew across 300 miles of the inland ice nobody saw so much as a square yard of it. Signals from the American radio beacon at Bluie West 8 told Mike he had crossed the cap and was over the fiordland of the west coast. He turned the Hastings north for Thule — still over grey-white cloud. But for the beacon signals and the navigator's plot they might have been anywhere. Then suddenly the cloud began to break up. Far below, sea littered with ice floes appeared, and away to starboard a great mass of mountains and glaciers. A big island passed below — Disko Island with the tiny settlement of Godhavn at its southern tip. They were now inside the Arctic Circle. The air was sparkling and clear and visibility only limited by the natural curve of the earth. Mike was astonished to find that he was able to identify landmarks on the coast 230 miles ahead. Beyond Upemavik the rugged coast they had been following began to recede away to starboard as they crossed Melville Bay. Below there was a narrow ice-free lane in the sea where a convoy of ships had recently forced a passage through the floes in the first attempt of the summer to reach Thule.

Ahead of the Hastings a range of snow-covered mountains showed up. It seemed a long time before the Hastings reached them, but when it did the mountains slid quickly by to reveal the biggest air base any of the crew had ever seen before. It was Thule, sprawling like some fantastic Wellsian city of the future over eighty square miles of bleak treeless fiordland. There was a huge crushed-rock runway, long enough to take the biggest aircraft in existence, big hangars, a network of roads along which a stream of trucks stirred up little puffs of dust, great stacks of equipment, a small fleet of ships nearby in the fiord, and most curious of all, hundreds of squat box-like aluminium buildings which glinted in the Arctic sunlight. Beyond, at the head of the valley past the ugly scars carved out of the frozen brown earth by the American construction gangs were mountains through which spilled the edge of the ice-cap itself. In the clear air the ice looked less than 2,000 yards away; in fact it was just fourteen miles.

Mike Clancy carefully circled the Hastings down into Thule's circuit. It was one of the most confusing circuits he had ever made, his judgment was grossly underestimating the true vastness of Arctic distance. From 5,000 feet the base had looked big enough but from circuit height it seemed to spread over ten times that area.

A reception party of U.S.A.F. officers was waiting for the Hastings when it landed. And so was an embarrassing moment for Clancy. A tall captain stepped forward who introduced himself as the base security officer. "Quite frankly," he said "we don't know what you guys are doing here. You had us worried back there. When our radar picked up an unidentified aircraft heading this way up the west coast we knew it wasn't one of ours and thought it must be either a Canadian Air Force ship or a Russian. But then we reckoned a Rusky wouldn't come from that direction so we just waited. By the time you dropped into the circuit here there was quite a bit of speculation on your identity. At first you looked like one of our C-54's, then when you put that tail wheel down and we saw there was no tricycle gear you should've seen our faces. You know, you had us guessing right up to a few minutes ago until we saw your markings and knew you must be British."

Mike was flabbergasted. "Didn't our people let you know we were coming?" he asked. The base security officer said it was quite likely. It was possible the message had been delayed somewhere. Meanwhile he would have to put a guard on the Hastings.

Later when Clancy went to park the aircraft — it was a three-mile journey to the dispersals — for the night he found a young Air Force police corporal sitting disconsolately inside. "I don't rightly know if you can come on board, sir," he said.

"But I'm the captain" exploded Mike.

The corporal said he didn't think that really mattered. His orders were that no one was to enter the Hastings.

In the end the security officer sorted it out. He told the unrelenting N.C.O. that Flight Lieutenant Clancy and Master Engineer Mosley were the only persons he could permit aboard until further orders. The S.O. said that anyone else with business aboard would carry a chit from him. At this the corporal looked worried. "But I don't know your signature, sir," he said. "Okay" said the S.O. — "here it is." He fished in his pocket, produced an empty cigarette packet, scribbled his signature on it and gave it to the security-conscious corporal. The Americans were taking no chances at Thule.

The British visitors stayed three days. And their American hosts having satisfied themselves that the unexpected guests were neither "Ruskies" nor saboteurs made them warmly welcome. For it was not everyday that an R.A.F. aircraft dropped in at this bleak base 900 miles from the Pole.

In Commander Simpson's plans for his two-year expedition the Americans were both intrigued and surprised. The acting base commander, small dapper pleasant and cigar-smoking to whom Commander Simpson put his requests for assistance in storing the equipment due by sea commented when first hearing details of the expedition: "Are you guys really going to sit up on that god-darned ice-cap for two years — its sounds plumb crazy to me. Anyway where's it going to get you?"

"We hope to learn a lot." Commander Simpson had said. "And our ice-cap station should be helpful to you here. We shall be radioing out weather reports."

The acting base commander agreed that this would indeed be useful. "A lot of our weather here comes straight off the cap," he said. "But just the same it isn't my idea of a holiday."

Nevertheless the Americans readily agreed to help the expedition in every way they could. They and Thule's Danish liaison officer, Commander Staermose promised to receive the equipment when it arrived, to arrange for walrus meat for the expedition's dogs, for fuel for the British snow weasels and for the use of the U.S.A.F. radio communications network to relay the expedition's messages when necessary. At the same time the two Transport Command officers made arrangements for the use of Thule by the R.A.F.'s supply dropping aircraft.

Meanwhile the R.A.F. crew were beginning to find their way around the big base. In the summer of 1952 Thule was still unfinished and seethed with construction activity. On all sides thousands of workers many of them veterans of American airfield projects in Okinawa, Guam, Alaska and Central America, were busy at work on this modern engineering miracle in the Arctic wasteland. Mike Clancy who as a married Flight Lieutenant in the R.A.F. was paid £1,100 a year and David Wright watched with envy the toil of bearded construction workers who for a ten-hour-day, seven-day week were receiving in some cases six times their pay. Some men were drawing 1,500 dollars a month: even janitors collected the equivalent of £75 a week. But for most of these 8,500 men the big pay lasted only for the five summer months to which the major activities were limited. Continuous darkness, temperatures down to 60 degrees below and winds of up to

120 miles an hour cut down much of the outdoor construction in Thule's winter.

While at Thule the R.A.F. men had their first close-up of the ice-cap. Here the inland ice sloped down to the coast and was only 1,200 feet above sea level. It spilled through the mountains at the head of the valley in which Thule lay and its cold white edge actually rested on the brown bog of the Arctic tundra. From the air base it looked a comfortable two-mile walk to the ice fringe. But they knew now that it was fourteen miles away. A truck drove them the first eleven miles and after that it was an hour's walk over the soft springy tundra to where the well defined edge of the cap began. Notices warned of the hidden perils of the seemingly innocent-looking ice, warned of concealed crevasses and advised sightseers not to wander far. For the ice-cap's crevasses are no miniature cavities. Narrow cracks, concealed by snow at the surface, they yawn hundreds of feet deep — and further inland where the cap rises, for thousands of feet. The Americans had good reason to be mistrustful of the smooth ice top; not long before a snow tractor with four men on board had plunged into a huge crevasse. Neither vehicle nor men were ever seen again.

The R.A.F. men walked a few yards onto the ice they had heard so much about, this ice which stretched away eastward in a silent gleaming unbroken plateau for 700 miles and which they were to see a great deal more of that summer. They didn't envy Commander Simpson and his men this frigid companion for two years; and they felt glad that their own association with it was to be a distant one from the warm cockpit of a Hastings. Although they were not to know it then some of them were to have a great deal more to do with the ice than they planned.

Each day they were at Thule there was something new to learn about life at this remarkable bastion of America's outer defence ring. For some time they had been puzzled as to why all the buildings were raised on wooden piles — like some ultramodern Malayan swamp village. The Americans explained that an arctic phenomenon called permafrost made this essential. Below the surface the ground was permanently frozen rock hard. The warmth from normal buildings transmitted through the structure would have melted the ice and the piles would slowly have sunk. To overcome this, buildings were erected on non-conducting wooden stilts and the floors insulated by thousands of hollow twelve-inch pipes. In summer the pipes were closed to keep warm air out, in winter opened to induce cold air in. In addition every building had to be anchored with concrete blocks; otherwise they would have been blown away: winds which swept down off the ice-cap were so violent that Thule, despite its proximity to the Pole, was virtually snow-free. As fast as snow fell it was simply whipped away.

There were two "climates" at Thule. Both could be felt within a few seconds of each other. One was outside, the other was indoors. Outside the wind which poured off the ice-cap was cold and penetrating. Inside — all buildings had two doors with an insulating air block between — air was steam-heated to near-tropical temperatures. In fact a man could retreat inside from a sub-zero atmosphere, peel off layer after layer of Arctic clothing and within a few minutes be reclining on his bed in only pyjama trousers — and still he was warm.

As Commander Simpson wanted to have a look at ice conditions at Britannia Lake, it was decided to fly the Hastings back across the ice-cap from Thule direct to Queen Louise Land and to head for Iceland from there. For the first 300 miles Mike flew in cloud. He flew at a safety height of 11,000 feet. The cap rose gently toward the centre from all sides like the roof of a great squat dome. It rose from about 1,400 feet near Thule to around 10,000 feet in the middle of Greenland although where the Hastings crossed it went no higher than 8-9,000 feet. An hour and a half out of Thule an excited voice shouted into the intercom: "There's the cap!" All eyes looked down. The Hastings was breaking out of the cloud and there 4.000 feet below was the brilliant white expanse of the inland ice. In every direction it stretched to the horizon, an unbroken breathtaking vista of virgin white, untarnished by even the smallest tree, the tiniest rock.

Commander Simpson came into the cockpit and stood between Clancy and Wright. He pointed down at the ice and said: "My future home. Next time I see this place I shall be down on the ice looking up."

From his warm seat, Mike looked down at the flat ice landscape where he knew the temperature was probably twenty or thirty degrees below freezing, and shivered. "I still prefer Ireland" he grinned. In front of him the radio altimeter flickered first around the 2,500 feet mark, then dropped to 2,400, 2,300, and soon to 2,000 feet. But all the while the Hastings was maintaining 11,000 feet above sea level. The radio altimeter measuring height above the ground confirmed that the level of the cap was steadily rising although it was imperceptible to the eye The only apparent break in the gleaming white sea were what looked like long shadowy ridges which occasionally passed below and stretched from horizon to horizon. Commander Simpson explained that they were not ridges. The only irregularity on the flat ice surface, he said, were the low furrows called *sastrugi* that were carved by the wind. The shadows that looked like ridges were in fact great yawning ice chasms, that reached for thousands of feet down into the cap. Their mouths were blocked with snow; they couldn't be detected from the ground. But from the air the snow appeared only as a shallow transparent covering.

To get a closer look at the cap, Mike descended to 100 feet above the ice. Down there it wore a vastly different appearance. A strong wind was driving a continuous veil of snow across the surface like dry sand on a windy beach and made the ice look as if in some uncanny way it was trembling; as if somehow it were alive. But at 100 feet Mike had to concentrate too much on his flying to take in much detail. The firm outline of the natural horizon was blurred by ice haze. He held the Hastings a safe distance above the snow by keeping the aircraft's shadow which flashed across the *sastrugi* ahead of him, the same apparent size. If the shadow grew bigger then the Hastings was getting too low and Mike would ease her back with a gentle back pressure on the control column. From 100 feet the snow-covered cap looked uncomfortably close. David Wright and Mike were sharing the same thought — how on earth they were going to judge a height of 30, 40, 50, or 60 feet or whatever dropping height was decided on over this eerie white void.

Back at safety height again the Hastings flew into more cloud and that was the last they saw of the cap that trip. The cloud stretched to the east coast and to Commander Simpson's disappointment blanketed Queen Louise Land and his base camp site at Britannia Lake. And now the radio began to bring them reports of bad weather over Iceland. Keflavik, their destination, reported driving rain, cloud down to ground level and fifty yards visibility. Deciding that a landing there under these conditions was too risky Mike chose, as he had adequate fuel, to overfly Iceland and go direct to Lyneham. But later when Flight Sergeant Burke made contact with the Scottish Air Traffic Control Centre at Prestwick he was advised that

Lyneham was fog-bound. It was suggested they land either at Prestwick or Valley, in Anglesey. Mike chose Prestwick. They landed after a thirteen-hour flight.

Mike handed Prestwick's duty weather officer a huge sheet of "met" observations they had made on the 2,700-mile flight. The "met" man accepted it eagerly. "Tooley," he said, reading it, "Where the hell's Tooley?"

CHAPTER 4

FEW maps of Greenland show the small five by two-mile stretch of muddy-coloured water that is Britannia Lake. Tucked away in the mountains of Queen Louise Land at Latitude 77° 10' N. and trapped at each end by big glaciers it had rarely if ever been seen by man before 1951 and certainly had no name to distinguish it from the hundreds of other desolate lakes in which the east Greenland coast abounds. But in less than three weeks in August 1952 this lonely little Arctic lake became the centre of one of the biggest operations Greenland has ever known. For seventeen days the barren brown mountains which surround it, echoed with the roar of four-engined flying-boats, the chugging of marine craft, the shouts of scores of men and the howl of dogs. And when on August 22 the last flying-boat flew away in gathering mist a small colony had appeared on its sandy shore; it was the headquarters of the British North Greenland Expedition and it was to stay there for two years.

Five Sunderland flying-boats of Coastal Command's No 230 Squadron made possible the establishment of the expedition at such an inaccessible spot. Before the summer of 1952 nobody knew for certain just how long Britannia Lake remained ice-free every year. Theoretically the brief warmth of the short Arctic summer should have melted the ice which covers the northern lakes for most of the year, leaving them clear enough for flying-boat operations for at least a month. It was reckoned that the lake would be clear of ice from mid-July to late August. Events showed that the theory was an over optimistic one. In fact, Britannia Lake opened its ice-bound doors to the

R.A.F. for less than three weeks. But it was long enough for 230 Squadron. In forty-five hectic sorties from Young Sound, on the coast 200 miles south, the squadron flew in almost the entire expedition, its huskies and 150 tons of supplies in a little publicised but very remarkable airlift.

Thirty-five-year-old Squadron Leader Jimmy Higgins, D.F.C., A.F.C. and Bar, 230 Squadron's Commanding Officer was in charge of the airlift. The operation order which he drew up called for forty aircrew and twenty ground staff to go to Young Sound. The idea was that four aircraft would load up from the supply ship *Tottan* in the Sound and take off for Britannia Lake each day at three-hour intervals. Take-off times were scheduled for 6 a.m., 9 a.m., noon and 3 p.m. This left a spare aircraft at Young Sound each day whose crew were to help a five-man Army detachment — commanded by Captain I. A. Luty, R.A.S.C. — with the loading and refuelling of the other four and give the servicing staff an opportunity to work on their own aircraft. Thus each aircraft and crew would fly to Britannia Lake and back daily for four days, have a day off the airlift and then do another four days' trips and so on. It was worked out that each flying-boat could carry three-and-three-quarter tons on each flight which needed forty-five sorties over ten or eleven days of uninterrupted flying. One of the squadron's biggest problems was how to transport the expedition's equipment — much of it bulky and very heavy — first from the shore at Young Sound where the *Tottan* was to establish a supply depot, out to the Sunderlands, and later, how to ferry it from the aircraft to the lake-side camp at Britannia Lake. Pontoons were necessary, too, so that the R.A.F. mechanics could work on the Sunderlands' engines while the aircraft were moored in the choppy water of the Greenland sound. The difficulty was fairly satisfactorily solved at Young

Sound by four heavy army pontoons and an eighteen-foot R.A.F. dinghy which the *Tottan* was to ship there. But no such arrangement could be made at Britannia Lake whose only link with the outside world was by air or sledge. In the end it was decided to dismantle a Saunders Roe pontoon at Pembroke Dock, fly it to Britannia Lake in two sections and there reassemble it. And to supplement this the expedition had two twelve-foot wooden dinghies built specially so that they could be squeezed through the door and satisfactorily stowed aboard a Sunderland. One of the dinghies was to have an outboard motor.

As a final addition to Britannia Lake's marine craft fleet it was arranged for a Lancaster of 210 Squadron to fly from St Eval in Cornwall and drop an R.A.F. airborne lifeboat into the lake. This lifeboat was to be used to tow pontoon loads of stores to and from the Sunderlands.

Squadron Leader Higgins flew the first Sunderland to Reykjavik on July 21. Commander Simpson and four members of the expedition went with him. Two days later the little Norwegian supply ship arrived. Jimmy Higgins and Commander Simpson went on board for a conference with the elderly captain for the Commander was anxious that a Sunderland should make a reconnaissance of Young Sound to ensure that it was ice-free before the *Tottan* sailed. But the seventy-three-year-old Norwegian had little faith in aerial ice spotting.

"For forty years I have sailed these waters without the help of aeroplanes," he insisted. "Why should there be reason for me to use them now. Ice or no ice I can find my way up the Greenland coast; for years I have been using the same route to Young Sound and always the sea is clear at the end of July."

He added that even if the Sunderland did make a reconnaissance of Young Sound he would prefer to disregard the report it brought back in favour of his own long experience inside the Arctic Circle.

However, despite the captain's mistrust of the new-fangled methods of Arctic voyaging Commander Simpson felt that for his own peace of mind he should have a look at the Sound. Bad weather delayed the reconnaissance for several days and the Sunderland was still waiting for a break in the weather when the independent little *Tottan* and her proud skipper cast off their moorings and headed out of Reykjavik for Young Sound. It was July 28 before the weather cleared and the flying-boat finally took off. Jimmy Higgins flew across Denmark Strait above cloud. They sighted Greenland near Scoresby Sound. Here the sky was clear, the sun was shining and the sound looked breathtakingly beautiful. It was Greenland's very brief summer and the coastal mountains had their lower slopes brown and snow-free; only the tops, painted with snow, gave any hint of the winter just passed during which a heavy snow blanket had lain over most of the country right to the edge of the sea — itself a sheet of frozen ice. But even in midsummer, Greenland's coast is never completely clear and the deep blue waters of Scoresby Sound were studded with gleaming white icebergs. Further out to sea the water was choked with pack-ice.

But the clear weather was not general. North of Scoresby Sound the Sunderland flew into a wall of cloud. Jimmy Higgins opened his four throttles and climbed. But the higher he went, the higher the cloud top rose ahead of him, until when his navigator called through the intercom that according to his reckoning they were over Young Sound, the altimeter was showing 9,000 feet. Outside the air temperature was at freezing-point and every time the flying-boat touched a cloud it was left with a layer of ice. There was nothing for it but to return to Reykjavik.

The following day came a jubilant signal from the master of the *Tottan*. Not only was he safely in Young Sound but, as he had predicted, the sound was free of ice.

A second Sunderland meanwhile had arrived at Reykjavik from Pembroke Dock and the following day both flying-boats flew to Young Sound and landed successfully near the *Tottan* whose crew were already hard at work unloading the expedition's stores. Those of the R.A.F. crew who waited for nightfall before climbing into their bunks aboard the Sunderlands that night were disappointed. When at one o'clock in the morning the sun was still shining over the mountains the full implications of the land of the midnight sun were brought home to them. Sleeping routines were to be badly disrupted for the whole time they were north of the Arctic Circle and there was an ever-present tendency to postpone bed-time until darkness that never came.

By August 3 all five Sunderlands were safely anchored in Young Sound. In the phenomenally clear visibility of the Arctic summer the sound looked at first much smaller than it in fact was. From the expedition's supply depot which was expanding daily beside the huts that were used by the 1950 Danish expedition, the sound looked about a mile wide, the mountains on the far side about 1,500 feet high. In truth the mountains were three and a half miles away and 4,500 feet high. Sunderland pilots who began by making super careful approaches to avoid the sheer cliffs that appeared to be a few feet from their wing tips were soon astonished to learn that there was room to takeoff *across* the sound with room to spare.

In those first few days of August the big Greenland sound buzzed with frantic activity. Pontoons, wooden craft and small yellow R.A.F. rubber dinghies shuttled between the ship, the flying-boats and the shore. Everybody worked like the proverbial black. Officers and men of the three Services sharing every task alike, struggled to stack the expedition's supplies into an orderly pile on the shingle beside the sound, supplies that were to support twenty-six men and thirty-six dogs for two long years. There were hut sections, coal, tons of tinned food, radio equipment, delicate scientific instruments, petrol and oil for the weasels, barrels of blubber — each weighing more than 400 lb each — and drums of dried fish for the huskies. Nor had the expedition overlooked the Christmas that it was to spend in its little prefabricated huts buried under twenty feet of snow. Heaviest of all single items was a big wooden crate weighing 540 lb; its label declared simply "Xmas Dinner — 1952".

The next stage of the operation was to get this huge pile of equipment to Britannia Lake. Success depended again on the condition of the lake. Was it yet free of ice? On August 3 Jimmy Higgins determined to find out. He took Commander Simpson in his own Sunderland — "O" for Oboe — and in company with Sunderland "Y" for Yoke flew north to Britannia Lake. Both aircraft carried a full load of stores. Ice signs en route were far from encouraging. At Dove Bugt, the big fifty-mile wide bay, forty miles east of Britannia Lake and in the narrow fiords leading off the bay the water was packed with ugly-looking icebergs. It was the same further inland at Seal Lake where Wing Commander Barret had landed the previous summer.

Over the Storstrømmen Glacier the Sunderland flew while all eyes peered ahead for the tiny pool of water that was Britannia

Lake. A few minutes later it came into sight. From shore to shore it was covered in ice. It was a bitter blow. Theoretically the ice should have melted a fortnight earlier. By early August it should have been well clear. But Greenland's northern lakes take no account of theory. Temperatures during the short summer allow only a narrow margin with which to melt the winter ice. And here at Britannia Lake the ice so far was winning. There was nothing for it but to return to Young Sound.

With Britannia Lake still ice-choked and the winter freeze due to set in within three weeks it looked as if the R.A.F. was going to have to fly a miniature Berlin airlift "round the clock" to get 150 tons of stores to the expedition's proposed base in time — presuming that the ice did melt. But Commander Simpson was cheerfully optimistic. "A lot can happen with the ice up here even in a week" he said. "We'll just have to be patient for a few days."

Meanwhile Jimmy Higgins, having had his first glimpse of the tiny lake he was expected to operate off, was having private misgivings as to the capability of the flying-boat to make a successful overshoot with nearly four tons of stores aboard should they ever have to make two attempts at landing. From the air the glaciers and mountains which surrounded the lake looked like dangerous obstructions to a heavily-laden aircraft struggling for height from a baulked landing. To satisfy himself Higgins decided to take all the pilots who had so far not seen the lake on a low level reconnaissance of it in an unladen aircraft. Taking Commander Simpson with them they took off at 8.30 a.m. on August 5. Ninety minutes later those back at Young Sound were startled to get a signal from the aircraft, "Preparing to land". Twenty minutes later a second message reported that the Sunderland was safely down on Britannia

Lake; in two days the ice had gone. For the R.A.F. men and the explorers it was a triumphant moment.

Up at Britannia Lake where all that remained of the ice of forty eight hours earlier were a few isolated bergs drifting in the middle of the lake, Squadron Leader Higgins was having trouble finding a spot that was shallow enough to anchor. The lake was immensely deep; even close to the shore, soundings made from the Sunderland's bow failed to find the bottom. In a rubber dinghy Squadron Leader Higgins, Commander Simpson and two others of the Sunderland's crew rowed ashore to look for a suitable site for the expedition's two-year base. Carrying the dinghy, they scrambled for half a mile round a steep rock-littered hillside until they came to a small stream. Where the stream bubbled into the lake there was a comparatively flat sandy shelf. Here, Commander Simpson decided, was the site for his camp. And from the dinghy the lead revealed a suitable anchorage for the flying-boats where the stream had silted up the lake. It was five fathoms 100 yards from the shore; beyond that the lake bottom shelved away suddenly to unfathomable depths.

A suitable camp site and anchorage having been found and fears of overshoot difficulties having proved groundless, everything was ready for the airlift to begin the following day. But fog which poured silently into Young Sound soon after the Sunderland's return from Britannia Lake reduced visibility to less than 150 yards and effectively "grounded" the flying-boats. It was not until August 7 that the weather cleared and the airlift was able to get under way.

Only two sorties were flown on the first day. But they got the Saunders Roe pontoons to Britannia Lake so that the receiving depot now had the means of ferrying cargo from the flying-boats to the shore.

This is how the airlift worked. The stores which the *Tottan* had put ashore at Young Sound were initially the responsibility of Captain Luty and his soldier assistants. It was essential for safe control of the aircraft that the loads were carefully distributed aboard and that they did not exceed the permissible weight for the 200-mile flight to Britannia Lake. And so Captain Luty had to weigh every single item from the half-hundredweight bags of dusty fuel and weasel tracks to barrels of strong-smelling fish for the dogs, and even the snarling huskies themselves. Not only did the equipment have to go aboard the aircraft according to weight; everything was handled in strict priority listed by Commander Simpson.

From the scales the stores went to a loading bay on the seashore, were manhandled onto pontoons and towed out across the often choppy water of the sound and stowed aboard the aircraft. It was an exhausting business, exhausting because every piece of equipment had to be heaved, or rolled or lifted by hand and there were all too few spare hands; even two newspaper men and an Air Ministry photographer who had come to Young Sound to record the airlift, soon found themselves hard at work lugging crates of food, hut sections and 380-lb barrels of weasel fuel.

Four times a day a Sunderland would roar off down the sound in a cloud of spray and climb away north with its heavy load. Very soon the mountain, glacier and fiord landmarks along the 200-mile route became as familiar to the pilots as the South Wales coast back at Pembroke Dock. As soon as they had landed at Britannia Lake the backbreaking work of unloading would begin. In the face of gale-force winds it sometimes took five hours and as soon as the Sunderlands had been emptied they would fly back to Young Sound. Every day there was fifteen tons less equipment left at the sound while at the northern lake the base camp grew proportionately bigger.

Unloading at Britannia Lake represented the biggest headache. The small craft which shuttled from aircraft to shore often in the teeth of bitterly cold forty-mile-an-hour winds which swept down the Unicorn Glacier off the ice-cap and whipped up four-foot high waves on the lake surface, suffered badly from engine trouble because of the intensely cold nights. And, after the airborne lifeboat on which all hopes were pinned, had been badly damaged in the dropping process, all of the equipment had to be hauled ashore on the pontoon with six men heaving at the end of a rope.

The day the Lancaster arrived and circled over Britannia Lake the British North Greenland Expedition very nearly lost its leader.

The Lancaster made its drop from 700 feet — the standard dropping height for the operation around Britain. But unfortunately on this flight moisture got into the parachutes and froze. The result was that some of the worst frozen canopies did not have time in such a short drop to unfreeze.

Only half of the parachute cluster attached to the lifeboat opened. Instead of floating gently down onto the lake the precious lifeboat went down at twice its scheduled speed and four feet of its bows broke off on impact. There were groans of disappointment at the base camp but despite the high wind Commander Simpson decided to attempt salvage.

With Lieutenant Angus Erskine, a member of the expedition and R.A.F. Sergeant Shelton-Smith he put out into the turbulent lake in a twelve-foot dinghy with an outboard motor. Flight Lieutenant C. M. Stavert, A.F.C., the pilot of the Sunderland in the lake at the time saw the little boat fighting its way out through big waves and decided to start his engines and slip moorings.

His action probably saved three lives, for a few minutes later the dinghy capsized in the high wind and the three occupants were flung into the freezing water. Kicking off their heavy boots they swam twenty yards to the waterlogged lifeboat and clambered aboard. Flight Lieutenant Stavert quickly taxied the Sunderland towards them and in a series of tricky manoeuvres drew alongside the derelict lifeboat. A line was passed to Commander Simpson from the flying-boat's rear door but the Commander, noticing that the parachutes which should have been automatically released themselves on landing, were still attached and acting as a sea anchor feared that the Sunderland might be damaged. He shouted to Erskine and Shelton-Smith to seize the line and jump for it. Erskine and the Sergeant were quickly hauled across to the flying-boat and pulled aboard through the rear door, but the Commander lost his grip. Immediately he was swept away and a few seconds later the men aboard the Sunderland could only get occasional glimpses of his head bobbing in the angry milky-coloured water. Somebody said: "*Christ!* He won't survive five minutes in that water", and Flight Lieutenant Stavert flung open his starboard outer throttle. Slowly the squat bulk of the Sunderland turned into wind and Stavert taxied off in pursuit opening and closing the throttles to swing the aircraft into position down-wind of the rapidly weakening Commander. Then using the wind as a break he motored slowly up to him. Up in the bows an R.A.F. man leaned out with a boat hook and as soon at the Commander was within reach hooked him by the collar. The end of the boat hook was passed down the side of the hull to the forward door and the expedition leader, almost unconscious with the cold, was hauled inside. He was the luckiest man in Greenland that afternoon.

On August 13 Sunderland "Victor" was returning to Young Sound from the lake when its starboard outer engine developed trouble twenty minutes after take-off. On three engines the pilot flew on to Young Sound where it was discovered that a replacement engine was necessary. This meant a flight to Reykjavik but as it was thought unwise to take off with a starboard engine out of commission the starboard outer and inner motors were swapped over. In the calm waters of Pembroke Dock with every facility available this would have been a major job. But in the boisterous water of this isolated Greenland sound with only the barest minimum of equipment at hand and a small swaying pontoon from which to work it was a Herculean task. And in the middle of the operation when all the pipes, rods and wires had been disconnected, two heavy starboard engines lowered onto the pontoon by a derrick rigged precariously on the wing and the serviceable inner motor raised up into the outer position, a violent sixty-mile-an-hour gale came howling through the sound. The flying-boat began to pitch, the pontoon rose and fell beside it like a cork and the loose engine about to be raised into position began to swing on its chains like a vicious pendulum. Frantically the fitters struggled to bring it under control but as they sweated and swore they didn't at first notice that something else was happening to Sunderland "Victor". It had dragged its moorings and was slowly drifting into deep water. But because the *Tottan* nearby had dragged her own moorings and the two were moving together the men furiously at work on the flying-boat weren't immediately aware of this. When the engine was at last in position they suddenly realized that they and the supply ship were heading for the cliff on the western side of the sound.

Unless something were done quickly it looked as if Coastal Command was going to lose an expensive aeroplane.

Back on shore where the gale was threatening to uproot the sleeping-tents, Squadron Leader Higgins rushed a party of pilots into a motor dinghy. After some difficulty the reluctant motor was coaxed into spluttering life. Alone the dinghy was incapable of towing twenty-seven tons of flying-boat so Higgins headed for the *Tottan* for help. But aboard the supply ship they were having trouble of their own. The engineer had no pressure with which to start his engines. So the men in the dinghy went over to the Sunderland and decided to make a desperate effort to take it in tow. The attempt failed but a few minutes later the master of the *Tottan* having found that one of his lifeboats could hold his ship into wind sent a whaler to the aid of the flying-boat, now only 100 yards from the shore and destruction. The combined efforts of the dinghy and the whaler just managed to hold the runaway Sunderland but even with their motors wide open, propellors flailing the water, were unable to draw the aircraft out into safe water. So Squadron Leader Higgins who had gone aboard started the starboard inner engine; but this only swung the aircraft nearer the shore. As a last resource some sandbags which had been stacked on the port wing during the engine change were dragged onto the starboard wing to that the starboard float dug into the water and the flying-boat stopped its shoreward swing. This saved the day. After a two-and-a-half hour haul the aircraft's engine and the two towing craft edged the Sunderland back to its moorings.

The airlift was now in full swing. Every day four, and sometimes six, flights were made to Britannia Lake and soon the pile of expedition stores beside the lake was bigger than at Young Sound. And all the while the question was on all lips:

"How long dare we keep the Sunderlands here?". The winter freeze was an unpredictable event — and once it set in the ice would be there to stay for another 11 months.

Squadron Leader Higgins worried about it most of all. He couldn't afford to gamble on the refreeze date, for the ice returned so suddenly that his Sunderlands could easily be trapped overnight and destroyed. The deadline he had been given was August 29 but when on the 18th "Victor" took off on three engines to return to Reykjavik it had to dodge big chunks of ice that the easterly wind was beginning to drift in from the open sea. Jimmy Higgins didn't like the look of these signs. He went over to see the master of the *Tottan* — *he* had been visiting Young Sound regularly for more than forty years.

The old Norwegian shook his head. "I do not think you are wise to stay here after the twenty-fifth," he said. "Some years the ice comes back on the thirtieth, sometimes on the twentieth, never can you tell. But the snow is a good warning. When the snow blows down from the glaciers then do we know that the sea here will be freezing very soon. Once the ice forms out at the entrance of Young Sound then the water here becomes still and quickly it freezes also." He said that on some of his past visits to Young Sound he had turned in at night with the sea peacefully lapping the side of his ship; next morning he had looked out of his porthole to find the whole sound coated with an inch of ice.

Later the Master's warning was confirmed from another quarter. A Canso of the Danish Air Force flew into the sound. Its pilot quickly knocked several more days off the safe deadline. If they were his Sunderlands, he said, he wouldn't get any sleep if they stayed in the sound much after August 22 or 23. In any case after that date they stood an excellent chance of being trapped in the sound by days of continuous fog.

As it was now the 18th it looked very much as if the R.A.F. would have to finish off the airlift quickly and get out. That day there were two signs that told everybody the airlift's days were numbered. The warning snow of which the Norwegian had spoken fell on the surrounding hills down to within 2,000 feet of the sea; a disquieting convoy of icebergs began to filter ominously in from seaward. And in the evening a monster berg two miles long and a mile wide came cruising sedately in. The Sunderland pilots looked at this floating ice-island with some horror, and were relieved when it stopped short of their anchorage. Squadron Leader Higgins held a hurried conference by radio with Commander Simpson at Britannia Lake and it was decided to rush the remaining stores — only thirty tons were left by this time — in eight immediate and successive sorties. Fortunately ice had not yet started to form at the lake.

Next morning, the 19th, the four Sunderlands were loaded faster than ever before, and each made two return trips to Britannia Lake. Up at the lake the Commander ordered every member of the expedition to turn to and help with the unloading. Late that night the last six tons of stores were safely ashore — but the two Sunderlands which had brought them were temporarily trapped at the lake by fog at Young Sound. And early next morning to the R.A.F. men's dismay the winter's first ice began to form round the aircraft on the lake. Things looked serious.

But the ice didn't stay long. During the day the Saunders Roe pontoon was dismantled and one half loaded on each aircraft. The flying-boat men said goodbye to the expedition and the two Sunderlands — the explorers' last link with civilization — whipped up the spray on Britannia Lake for the last time and climbed away south.

230 Squadron's work in Greenland was completed — but for one final task. Commander Simpson had asked for small loads of supplies to be parachuted at three points in Queen Louise Land which they planned to visit later in the summer, and a fourth load to a detachment of the expedition who were waiting near Seal Lake for the *Tottan* to land the eight weasels late in August on the nearby coast at Walrus Point inside Dove Bay.

(Pack ice subsequently prevented the *Tottan* from reaching Walrus Point and the weasels were unloaded on the coast at Kap Rink, 150 miles further south. Later when the ice hardened they were driven north to the Danish weather station at Danmarkshavn on the coast east of Seal Lake. They were driven across the Storstrømmen Glacier to Britannia Lake for use on the ice-cap in the spring of 1953.)

Conditions were rapidly deteriorating at Young Sound where three Sunderlands remained — another had by now returned to Reykjavik. No longer could the R.A.F. depend on continuous daylight; several hours of Arctic twilight were setting in. Long fingers of fog were starting to seep into the sounds and fiords, heavy snow showers began to blow down off the inland ice, thick rime ice began to form on the tents and huts ashore and, worst of all, icebergs were now rolling up the sound in alarming and persistent squads. The huge two-square mile berg was still uncomfortably close to the moorings and house-sized chunks began to break away from it and drift towards the helpless aircraft.

The crew of "Zebra" had a specially nasty moment when in the early morning twilight one ugly fragment fifty feet long and thirty feet across set a relentless course for the aircraft. There was a swift scramble to man all the flying-boats and for the next half hour the sound echoed with the roar of Sunderlands taxiing to safer positions. To add to the confusion a heavy fog layer had now settled over the water and nobody was quite sure just how many bergs were filtering in. The big fragment, however, was too close to be comfortable so a party manned a dinghy and set off to intercept it. Attempts at digging a grappling iron into its four-foot high sides failed so one of the party scrambled onto the slippery floe and forced the iron into the middle. Anyone arriving at Young Sound that morning would have been startled to see looming up through the eerie gloom of the Arctic night, a dinghy load of Royal Air Force officers and airmen crawling down the sound towing a big unwilling iceberg.

Fog cloaked the sound until after midday on the 21st and when sluggishly, it lifted sufficiently for "Zebra" and "Yoke" to take off on the two paradropping missions the pilots saw that very little of Young Sound was left free of ice. It was clear that all the aircraft would have to be out of the place within twenty-four hours at the latest.

"Yoke" dropped supplies at three points. The first was beside a small peak which poked out of the edge of the ice-cap — *nunataks* they are called in Greenland — where Commander Simpson wanted a depot for his journey to the site of the proposed winter ice-cap station, a sledge trek he and five others had already begun. This depot, 5,000 feet above the base camp, was vital to the Commander's ice station plans, for his dogs could not haul heavy loads up the tortuous Unicom Glacier from Britannia Lake and unless supplies were dropped at some intermediate point he would be unable to continue his march across the ice-cap to the point in central Greenland where Topcliffe's Hastings were to sustain him from Thule.

Two members of the expedition, Lieutenant Graham Rollitt, a meteorologist and Peter Taylor a glaciologist had left

Britannia Lake three days before to climb the Unicorn Glacier to the edge of the ice-cap and receive the Sunderland's drop. But for two days a violent gale had streamed off the ice-cap and Rollitt and Taylor had huddled storm-bound in their tiny tent in the snow among the sea of crevasses where the ice, cracked and wrinkled begins to spill down into the glaciers of Queen Louise Land.

And so the crew of "Yoke" circled the black rock outcrop searching for signs of the men below in vain. In the end they pushed the ton load out in two separate clusters of parachutes and hoped that the stores would be found before the gale carried them into crevasses. Then the Sunderland flew south to another *nunatak* which Commander Simpson had named Selsey Bill, dropped a smaller load for another expedition reconnaissance party and then east to diminutive newly-discovered Trident Lake, with a third bundle. An hour and a half later "Yoke" was back at Young Sound. Meanwhile "Zebra" was dropping supplies to the detachment at Seal Lake. One of the loads, a bulky box weighing three hundredweight gave the crew a bad moment. It was only after great difficulty that they got it through the aircraft's bomb doors — in the Sunderland on the side of the fuselage under the wing — only to have the slipstream wham it back jamming it rigidly half in, half out. Two, three, four of the crew grunted, cursed and heaved; the obstinate box pinned by the pressure of the slipstream would not budge. A fifth and a sixth man lent their weight and invective, to no avail. Finally seven despatchers and crew using all the strength and oaths they could muster released the box and sent it gliding majestically down toward Seal Lake.

Next day when Squadron Leader Higgins and his crew came out of their tents at Young Sound the aircraft out at their moorings were concealed in cold grey fog. It looked far from promising for the take-off back to Reykjavik and England. It was August 22. Barely four weeks earlier had Greenland shaken off her winter mantle and opened her doors to the intruders from the outside world. And now everywhere there were signs that those frigid doors were closing again. Greenland's summer was over and already the sun low on the horizon was failing to break through the fog and disperse it. At midday the Sunder-lands were still fogbound in the sound. Thirty-five R.A.F. men and five Army men were all wondering the same thing. Had they overstayed their visit, had the fog now come to stay, was the door closing on them?

But at 12.30 somebody yelled; "It's lifting". It was only a temporary, patchy clearance, but it was long enough for Squadron Leader Higgins in "Oboe". His Sunderland roared away in a curtain of spray and fog and they heard him climbing away safely towards Iceland. Now the fog began to roll in again. The two other captains decided that there was no time to be lost if they were to see their squadron commander again that year.

Flight Lieutenant Cassels in "Yoke" set a compass course from near the *Tottan* and taxied down the sound to check that Squadron Leader Higgins' misty take-off path was still free of ice. As he taxied he had to dodge small ice floes which slid past his floats. The further he went the more floes there were, until finally a low wall of pack ice loomed up in front of him and he knew that the only reasonably clear water in the sound was now behind him. Between this advancing barrier and the *Tottan* Flight Lieutenant Cassels decided there was room to take-off.

He went back to the ship pointed the Sunderland down the sound, edged open his four throttles then as he had no visual horizon to keep him straight on take-off he transferred his attention to his blind flying panel and took off on instruments.

Just as their hull kissed the last wave and the flying-boat crept into the air a gasp went through the intercom as the pack ice wall flashed below just a few feet under the aircraft. A minute later "Yoke" was above the fog in brilliant sunshine. Looking back at the mountains waist deep in fog the crew hoped that "Zebra" would be as fortunate as they.

Back in the sound Flight Lieutenant Stavert had taxied to the take-off point but before he could get off a clammy belt of fog closed in and he couldn't see more than a few yards in any direction. For three quarters of an hour he taxied carefully up and down praying for just one final break while the crew were making gloomy mental plans of the winter it looked as if they might have to spend there. Down the sound a shaft of sunlight stabbed through the fog; miraculously a clear tunnel opened up in the grey blanket. A minute later "Zebra" was airborne. All the Sunderlands had escaped. Next day when the aircraft were well on their way back to Pembroke Dock, Young Sound froze from shore to shore. And the *Tottan* had to force a route through the ice to get out.

CHAPTER 5

FIVE thousand feet up, on the crevassed edge of the icecap above Britannia Lake six members of the British North Greenland Expedition were en route with three dog teams to establish the ice-cap station. It was August 26. With Commander Simpson were Graham Rollitt, Peter Taylor, Richard Hamilton, Angus Erskine and Ken Taylor. After the station was set up — it was planned to put it exactly where the 78th Parallel cut the 40th Meridian, about 250 miles west of Britannia Lake — Rollitt and the two Taylors were to remain there for the winter and the others would sledge back to the lake.

Hull-born Graham Rollitt who was to command the lonely ice station during the long months of blizzards and darkness was thirty-two. An Instructor Lieutenant in the Navy he had been a Fleet Air Arm pilot during the war and had since trained as a meteorologist. Twenty-nine-year-old Ken Taylor, a Navy Petty Officer telegraphist was to maintain the ice station's radio through which daily contact would be made with Britannia Lake. Third and youngest member of the icecap team was Peter Taylor. One of the expedition's glaciologists, he had packed a great deal into his twenty-five years. A qualified naval architect he had already taken part in two expeditions to Iceland and had led a third to Norway.

A graduate of Dartmouth Royal Naval College Lieutenant Angus Erskine, a twenty-four-year-old Scot was the expedition's "Officer i/c Dogs". He had spent the previous winter at Jakobshavn in west Greenland buying the huskies and learning to sledge. Dr. Richard Hamilton was second in command, senior meteorologist and Chief Scientist of the expedition. No stranger to Greenland, he could claim to be one of the few men who had found a wife in the Arctic. Thirteen years before, in 1939, he had been a member of a three-man expedition to north-west Greenland. At Thule he fell in love with the governess to the local governor's children. Later they were married.

It was an immense relief to Commander Simpson, five days from Britannia Lake, to find most of the supplies dropped by the Sunderland near the rocky outcrop of the *nunatak*, intact.

At first when they found one of the parachuted loads two miles from the *nunatak* they had feared that if one could have blown so far from the dropping zone, the others might be widely scattered. But after two days' searching and collecting they were delighted to find that, despite losses, they had enough food for men and dogs for forty-five days. For the first time they knew for certain that they could go forward on their journey.

At the end of the first week in September, signals from Commander Simpson relayed to London through Britannia Lake reported that the ice-cap party, which had been sledging steadily westward at about fifteen miles a day, was more than half way to the 40th Meridian. It was time for the Hastings to leave.

Mike Clancy in Hastings WD 492 left Lyneham for Thule at 8 a.m. on September 9. Squadron Leader Eric Robinson, the detachment commander, flew the aircraft. David Wright followed in WD 490 half an hour later. At Lyncham Mike had picked up Major Barker-Simson, four Army despatchers and an Air Ministry photographer, Mr. Finbow, who was soon to acquire the descriptive nickname "Scoop".

After a night stop at Keflavik both aircraft flew across the southern ice-cap and up the Greenland west coast to reach Thule the following afternoon. It was only three months since the two R.A.F. pilots had made their proving flight but in that time Thule's construction army had been busy. Scores more buildings had gone up, the runway had been resurfaced and a small mountain which had been a prominent landmark twelve weeks earlier had almost been levelled flat.

With memories of his last surprise arrival fresh in his mind, Mike taxied across to the base operations building with some trepidation. But by now their business was well-known. The base security officer said: "The last time you guys dropped in here we hadn't a clue who you were. But when the captain said his name was Clancy, why we were sure the whole thing was phoney". Mike was to discover that nobody at Thule would seriously believe his name was Clancy. It was a blow to Irish dignity but the truth was that to the Americans Clancy was the canine hero of a cartoon strip and nothing else. His name remained a constant source of entertainment there.

The base security officer briefed the R.A.F. detachment on Thule's security regulations and told them where and where not they could wander. Much of Thule was still a closely guarded secret and large areas of the base were out-of-bounds. Then the R.A.F. were shown their quarters in the superheated sleeping blocks where the temperature — between 70° and 80° — prompted someone to remark: "Blimey, it's worse than ruddy Singapore". During the first night while some of the R.A.F. men, stripped to the waist, tossed and turned sleepless through heat one enterprising Englishman crept out to the block heat regulator and gave it a smart twist in the "off" direction. Slowly the temperature dropped back through the seventies and sixties and the sound of heavy slumbers began to issue from the R.A.F. rooms. Suddenly there was a bedlam of irate American voices, doors opened and closed, footsteps hurried down the passage, the regulator was jerked back on and soon the hothouse atmosphere had returned.

Thule's base commander, Colonel Robert Humphreys, appointed a "project man" to be liaison officer between the R.A.F. detachment and the Americans. He was Captain Charles W. Stover, a cheerful ex-fighter pilot with close-cropped hair. Only thirty-four he was considered too old to fly fighters any longer and was doing a maintenance job at Thule. "Just call me Smokey", he told the Hastings pilots.

The eighty tons of stores which the Hastings were to drop had arrived safely by sea and the R.A.F. men got busy helping Major Barker-Simson and his loading team to uncrate and repack it in suitably sized loads for air dropping. Eighty tons is not a colossal amount of equipment but to the small British detachment sorting the hundreds of different items in the order the expedition wanted it, repacking, weighing, loading and delivery to six men who could only be expected to receive limited quantities at a time, represented continuous hard work.

With each Hastings making one sortie a day carrying around three and three-quarter tons it was reckoned that the job would take about twenty days. Everything required to house and feed for six months three men living in the middle of an ice desert had to be dropped. The hut in which they were to live was to be supplied in sections and was first on the dropping priority list. The idea was that the expedition could begin erecting it immediately and so have to spend as little time as possible in the cramped space of their tents. Other stores to be dropped included a 650-lb generator, hundreds of jerrycans of petrol and diesel oil for the weasels — due up from the east coast the following spring — kerosene, gear oil, spare weasel tracks, cylinders of Calor gas, explosives, sledges, nearly half a ton of dog food, radio spares, batteries, films, clothing, a stove complete with chimney, meteorological instruments, medical kit, cooking utensils, thousands of cigarettes, flour, tea, sugar, rice, dehydrated potatoes, soya beans, dried fruit, rum, and even a small consignment of beer.

Six hundred miles east of Thule a cluster of tiny specks was moving slowly westward toward the centre of the ice-cap.

It was a hard, wearying journey in the face of blinding blizzards, fraught with the insidious perils of frostbite and the ever-present dangers of devilishly concealed crevasses, into which a whole team could disappear, man, sledge and all without trace. How did these six modern explorers feel facing many of the hardships, and cold as great, if not greater, than that experienced by their more celebrated predecessors on the high plateau of the south Pole?

As they sledged westward the mountains of Queen Louise Land sank slowly below the horizon behind them and their lonely little procession became the only dark object in a sea of white.

For the first few days the surface of the cap undulated in sympathy with the land over which it lay, but further away from the coastal mountains where the ice was thousands of feet deep is assumed an almost perfect flat top with a very gentle upward slope toward the west. Down this slope into their faces swept an icy wind; it bit deep into bare flesh that was left uncovered and kept the temperature at between 0° and 10°F.

At first the snow surface was good; the six men made encouraging progress. But on September 1 the little cavalcade ran into an area of soft deep snow. Worse, beneath the feathery snow great crevasses began to cross their route. They couldn't see these dangerous clefts in the ice below; the only indication of their whereabouts was when a sledge suddenly burst through the surface snow and hung poised either across the crevasse or perched precariously on the edge of it. Sometimes the snow was so insecure over a chasm the sledges would have to be unloaded to prevent them falling through.

In three days they made a bare ten miles, ten painful miles which took a great deal out of the dogs, and left several of them badly weakened. One of Angus Erskine's team just lay down in its tracks. Nothing could persuade it to move; ten minutes later it was dead.

The second day in this area was Commander Simpson's birthday. His present from each of his five companions was a bar of chocolate and in their tent that evening they celebrated the occasion with an iced birthday cake brought from England.

At last they reached a region of firmer snow. For a week they made good progress but their troubles were not over. On September 10 it became suddenly much colder; the temperature fell to — 19°F and a near-blizzard howled down on them. It was so fierce the dogs almost refused to face it and the men themselves had to lean forward with their parka hoods pulled tight round their faces. Few of them escaped slight frostbite that day.

On September 12 the temperature rose again and the wind abated slightly. But the journey was beginning to tell on the dogs. It was clear that many more miles would mean big sacrifices in the teams. One of the Commander's bitches became so weak they had to destroy her. And then as if nature was trying to help, another bitch suddenly produced a tiny furry pup; but it lived only a few seconds.

Next day two more dogs died. The trouble was that the expedition's dogs had not been as fit as they might have been at the start of the journey. They had lost condition badly during the long sea voyage from west to east Greenland the previous month. By September 13 when the ice-cap party had sledged to within 30 miles of their planned position at the 40th Meridian the Commander was seriously considering going no further.

On September 13, Squadron Leader Robinson, decided it was time to fly a reconnaissance over the ice-cap, establish the Commander's position and drop food to put new life into the flagging huskies. Mike Clancy took off in WD 492 and Reg Michie gave him a course to the position of the proposed icecap station at Latitude 78°N, Longitude 40°W. For two-and-a-half hours the Hastings flew east in clear sunny weather, 2,000-feet above the shimmering ice sea. There were no landmarks to help them and Reg and second navigator Les Richardson worked hard at their charts computing courses by dead reckoning from the limited information at their disposal — radio back bearings near Thule and shots of the sun which hung low and orange over the southern horizon.

But when the pencil line on Reg's chart had crept out to 78°N, 40°W and he called up Mike to tell him they were there, there was nothing below but ice; not a speck as far as could be seen from 2,000 feet. For half-an-hour as they square-searched they called the Commander on the radio asking him where he was but there was no reply; the six men were on the move, their radio was packed away and the only sound they heard was the yapping of huskies and the roar of the freezing wind in their parka hoods. So Mike decided to fly on to Britannia Lake, call up the base camp and get information about the Commander's position from them.

At the base of the great Unicorn Glacier they found the muddy brown pool of Britannia Lake but had difficulty spotting the camp. However, the expedition's radio operator said they could hear and see the Hastings, so Mike asked for a smoke signal. A minute later a small column of smoke rose from the north side of the lake and the men in the air saw at the foot of it a collection of orange painted huts and a big pile of stores. Mike circled the Hastings carefully down between the mountains and roared over the lake at 800-feet. It was the first aircraft the expedition had seen since the Sunderlands left and they gave it a great welcome. Men came out of the huts and waved frantically, someone fired off a string of red Verys and over the radio excited voices asked many questions.

Given the Commander's latest position, Mike circled up and flew back westward to renew the search for the ice-cap party. The six men were in fact thirty miles short of their intended ice station position; they were at 78°7'N, 38°10'W. Mike approached this position from the east making a "creeping line-ahead search" — flying a zigzag track left and right of what they hoped was Commander Simpson's route. When they reached a point which the navigators estimated was within ten miles of his position the Arctic twilight began to set in and soon it was nearly dark. Knowing that the party would now have pitched camp for the night, Mike tried to call them on the radio again.

Immediately a voice came back; it was the ice-cap party, talking from one of their tents into which they had just crawled, weary from a hard day's sledging. Presently the tired voice of the Commander came up to the aircraft. His dogs were in such a poor condition, he said, that he was tempted to establish his ice station where he was. He had already lost too many dogs and he feared that the two or three day's sledging necessary to reach the exact position of 78°N, 40°W might kill more than he could afford to sacrifice; he was dependent on the dogs to get Erskine, Dr. Hamilton and himself back to Britannia Lake a few weeks later.

Although the strength of the Commander's radio indicated that the Hastings was very near to the two tents half-an-hour's search failed to find them. Red Verys from the aircraft went arcing out into the grey twilight but the men on the snow didn't see them; nor could they hear the drone of the Hastings. In the grey void of the ice-cap it was all too easy for two parties to slide past within a few miles of each other without sight or sound of each other.

So Mike flew back to Thule to await Commander Simpson's decision on the final position of his station. He left the lonely little tents in approaching darkness but flying west with the sun landed at Thule three hours later in bright sunshine.

Next day, Sunday, September 14, the Commander signalled Thule through Britannia Lake that he had decided to remain where he was; supply dropping could begin immediately. Twenty-four days after leaving Britannia Lake the explorers had come to the end of their journey; they were nearly in the middle of Greenland. To celebrate they served out extra rations and relaxed from the discipline of the trail. And that evening all six of them crowded into one small tent for Evensong, and held their first service together, giving thanks for a safe arrival. Seven hundred miles from the Pole, 220 miles west of Britannia Lake and 480 miles east of Thule the two tents, against whose flapping walls the Greenland wind was already beginning to raise a bank of dry, powdery snow, represented the only interruption, the only black dots on the

700-mile wide ice sea. "Northice", for that was the name Commander Simpson had decided to give his icy outpost, was ready to expand.

CHAPTER 6

IT WAS David Wright in Hastings 490 who made the first drop to Northice. With the big double doors removed from the port side he took off with a load of hut sections and headed out over the ice-cap. For two-and-a-half hours they cruised eastward wondering if their navigation was going to be good enough to find the specks on the snow. But soon after Wright's navigator, Brian Adlington, looked up from his charts and announced; "We should be there", two tents and the tiny figures of men beside them obligingly loomed up ahead. It was an excellent bit of navigation.

For an-hour-and-a-half the Hastings circled the dropping zone which the ground party had marked out with strips of red and yellow cloth not far from their tents and the hut sections went floating down in thirty parachute loads. A few of the chutes failed to open and the precious hut boards smacked heavily down into the snow. Mercifully, however, the soft shifting snow which covers the ice, cushioned the impact and none was damaged. The only exception was the special Arctic-type double-walled chimney; it was squashed flat beyond all hope of repair.

After paradropping, David Wright brought the Hastings in at fifty feet for a trial free drop of three bundles. The loads whisked out and almost before the slipstream could whip them away were bouncing on the snow — intact. Commander Simpson was very relieved for much depended on the success of this method of dropping. So far so good.

Next day, September 16, it was Mike Clancy's turn. They didn't know it then but it was to be 492's last flight of all; a one-way trip to Northice and no return.

Eleven others flew with Mike that fateful morning. In addition to Adair, Michie, Richardson, Mosley, Burke and Boyd — his crew — there were five others. Major Barker-Simson who hadn't missed a sortie so far decided to go along and help his despatches; the despatches that day were Corporal Brian Yates a big Northumbrian lad, Corporal Brian Fussey a young Army photographer and a little Welsh Private with a thin moustache, "Taffy" Jones. Twelfth man was Smokey Stover. The night before he had approached Clancy in the mess and said: "You know Mike, I think I'll come along with you tomorrow and have a look at this thing from the air". And Mike had said: "Sure, you're very welcome". Stover said that he would lend a hand with the despatching.

They had breakfast, the twelve of them, at 4.30 a.m. for the time difference between Thule and Northice required an early start. The expedition was keeping Greenwich Time which was four hours ahead of Thule time. Over in the operations room the duty officer was preparing a weather forecast for the flight, based on early morning reports radioed from Northice through Britannia Lake. They were not encouraging. Commander Simpson said there was a surface wind gusting up to twenty-five knots whipping up loose snow. Surface visibility was seven miles and a heavy overcast hung 2,500 feet above the cap.

At Thule conditions were worse. A fifty-knot gale howled down the valley bringing sporadic stinging blizzards of windblown snow from off the inland ice. But between the snow showers there were brief clearances when visibility increased to ten miles. Mike decided to get off in one of these periods.

It was seven o'clock when the Hastings, heavily laden with hut sections and jerrycans of petrol pointed its nose down Thule's long runway. So strong was the wind that the four throttles had barely been opened when the tail came up and 492 struggled into the air. There was some unpleasant buffeting until they crept clear of the coastal mountains but soon they rose through a belt of grey cloud and broke out into glorious sunshine. But it was only temporary.

Over the ice-cap at 7,000 feet they flew into thick cloud which persisted for the next 100 miles. An hour out of Thule, now at 11,000 feet, the Hastings suddenly came into the clear again but here the air was hazy with ice crystals through which the sun shone only with an eerie watery glow. The ice haze destroyed the natural horizon of the white cap below and all the pilots could see in any direction was a white nothingness in which ground and sky merged in one white blur. It seemed almost too much to expect to find two insignificant little tents in this vast empty white world. But soon Reg Michie announced that they were within twenty miles of the camp. Mike began a gentle descent to within 1,500 feet of the cap and now they began to make out the *sastrugi* lanes on the snow and were relieved to see the thin hazy outline of the ice horizon around them. From the cockpit Mike and Ted strained their eyes for a glimpse of even the tiniest speck on the endless white carpet below, but all they saw was their own faithful black shadow flashing along beside them over the snow. Soon the two pilots were seeing imaginary tents, men and dogs everywhere they looked; tension in the cockpit grew. And presently, when Reg came up on the intercom to say that if they hadn't spotted Northice they must have overflown it, Mike decided to begin a square search. He also called the elusive camp on R/T … "Northice, this is Baker Uncle. Do you read, over".

Almost immediately a voice crackled back into his helmet: "Hello Baker Uncle, this is Northice reading you strength three". The ground set had only a five-to-ten-mile range so they were getting close. Outside the landscape was still flat white and featureless. There were no helpful radar blips on Les Richardson's Rebecca screen although it had been one of the aids planned to home the aircraft onto the dropping zone, nor were there any reassuring signals from the radio beacon with which the ice-cap party should have been equipped. Their only aid was the cheerful voice on the short-range R/T and now that was rapidly fading.

Mike turned the Hastings back in the direction the radio was calling from and presently the voice of Petty Officer Taylor came in again faintly at first and then louder. And just as Mike was after asking the spalpeens of explorers to put up some smoke or poop off a few reds there came a jubilant shout on the radio: "We can see you."

They appeared to be about three miles away on the horizon, Taylor said. Then he called: "Turn port", followed a minute later by "straighten up, we are now dead ahead of you". The two pilots peered ahead and there sure enough looming out of the white mist was Northice — two proud little tents, a small stack of equipment, a cluster of dogs and several figures moving nearby. From three miles away they looked like dust specks on a big white table cloth.

As the Hastings ran in over the camp Commander Simpson's clipped voice came on the radio with a word of greeting for Mike. "How very nice so nearly to see you again", he said.

Mike made a wide circle and brought the Hastings down to as near as he could judge was 1,000 feet above the cap. His altimeter indicated 9,347 feet above sea level. He decreased power, lowered thirty degrees of flap and slowly the Hastings speed dropped from 175 to 130 knots.

Down on the snow a man was waving; but the others, bent against the wind were hard at work with a sledge collecting the hut sections which had been dropped the previous day. Mike wondered why they showed so little interest in the aircraft; later he was to learn that for good reason they were deliberately not looking up into the sub-zero wind.

Back in the fuselage Major Barker-Simson was supervising the supply stacking. Through the open door the freezing slipstream swept bringing numbing cold and the deafening roar of the four engines. Presently the major whose moustache had become stiff with ice, called Mike on the intercom: "First load ready and stacked".

Downwind on his circuit Mike lost height to the correct paradropping height, 800 feet. Taylor called up: "Ready for your first load". Michie left his plotting table behind the pilots and crawled down into the nose to give aiming directions. Stretched out on his stomach he switched on the circuit of indicating lights with which he communicated with the despatches.

The Hastings turned into wind. The bright red fluorescent panel marking the beginning of the dropping zone glinted through the white haze. Michie flicked a switch. "Red light on" he called through the intercom.

At the open door five pairs of eyes were fixed on the indicator bulbs. One glowed dull red. Barker-Simson bracing himself against the blast of the slip-stream called back: "Red light on". The soldiers tightened their grip on the first load of hut sections. Five seconds crawled by. Then from the nose came a terse "Green light on". The red bulb went out and the green lit up. "Green light on" acknowledged Barker-Simson. The despatches heaved the load through the door — it was snatched away and behind the Hastings a cluster of parachutes floated down onto the snow.

"Green light off" ... "Green light off". Mike opened the throttles and climbed back to 1000 feet while the radio announced "That was quite a nice drop".

Twelve times Mike ran in over the camp until the white dropping zone was speckled with supplies and coloured parachutes. One load — it was a spare Eureka beacon — was blown away by the wind. The parachute didn't collapse on landing as it should have done and the pilots were amused to see it bowling off over the ice-cap with a man on a sledge furiously driving his dog team in pursuit. But the renegade load had a good start and quickly disappeared into the hazy distance. On their next circuit the crew saw the sledge-man returning empty-handed. With not even the smallest ice-hillock to bar its way the load was probably five miles away, still going strong.

Now it was time for the trickiest part of the operation, the free drop from fifty feet. It was a new experience for both pilots and as Mike made his preliminary circuit he wondered how the difficult business of precision height judging was going to work out. The weather wasn't going to help him. Ground-level visibility had been about four miles when they had arrived at Northice; now it was down to two miles and the horizon was only faintly visible as a thin hard-to-define line in the grey-white haze which lay over the cap.

Relaying his instructions to the ground through signaller Burke, Mike told the Commander he was coming in to free-drop jerrycans of petrol and oil. The ground replied that they were ready and would "talk" the aircraft down as it lined up for the run in. Mike called Michie out of the nose and Adair now took the job of drop aimer using an auxiliary set of indicator switches in the cockpit — it was too dangerous to have a man in the nose for such a low run.

On his downward leg two miles from the tents, Mike made a gradual descent from 800 to 250 feet. The snow began to look very, very close. No longer was it a shapeless white plateau; it was now bristling with an immense amount of shivering detail; the long wind-blown *sastrugi* behind which the sun, low on the horizon, threw soft grey shadows, began to come alive while over the furrows slid an endless stream of loose powdery snow.

Barker-Simson's reassuring voice was on the intercom — "First load stacked and ready". At 200 feet the Hastings turned in toward the dropping zone. Mike decreased power on the inboard engines and the airspeed indicator crept back to 145, 140, 135 knots. The speed too was a vital factor now; it had to be low to avoid damaging the stores yet at this height it couldn't be allowed to drop too near the stalling point.

Ted Adair began calling out the decreasing airspeed. "132 … 130 … 128" he was chanting. Mike noticed that there were white icicles hanging from Ted's mask. It was getting cold, despite the cockpit heating. At 100 feet the radio altimeter suddenly began erratically flicking about the dial; it swung from 50 feet to 200 feet then trembled inconsistently in between. It was reading *through* the surface snow to the level of the hard ice below and was dangerously unreliable. Mike disregarded it and flew on his sensitive altimeter — it was an aneroid and unaffected by the nature of the ground.

Ahead, a kaleidoscope of tents, stores, men and dogs was rushing toward them. And beside the radio tent in which Petty Officer Taylor was talking to the aircraft, Commander

Simpson stood in the snow, eyes glued to the Hastings, shouting his estimates of its height. Above the noise of the aircraft he called: "Tell them they're coming in nicely at 80 feet". Mike decided to hold this height and glide off the last 30 foot over the D.Z. And then Adair's quiet voice was saying "Red light on ... green light on", the despatchers gave the platform a heave, and a load of jerrycans whammed down into the snow. "Green light off". Mike edged the throttles forward, gently to avoid throwing the men behind off-balance, the Hastings steadied and climbed away. "That was a nice drop", the radio was saying. "You were about eighty feet". Mike had noticed the exact reading on his altimeter — 8,427 feet. Knocking 30 foot off this he would make his next run at precisely 8,397 feet. If the men on the snow had estimated correctly this would bring him over the D.Z. at bang on 50 feet.

For the second time the Hastings swept in. The Commander called up to ask them to make the drop a little to one side of the last. He was afraid the jerrycans might smash onto those already lying in the snow.

They came in from two miles downwind, this time at 50 feet. Adair was calling out the airspeed again "128 .... 126 .... 126 .... 124" — too low — a touch of power — "125.... 126 .... 126".

Now the snow was zipping past, not only below but all around them; they were so low the ice-cap seemed to be *above* them. From the fuselage door the despatchers had a sort of train window view of a snow-covered landscape and Major Barker-Simson yelled to Smokey Stover: "Good Lord, you can put your foot out and drag it on the snow". Ten seconds later they were all on the snow.

A lot happened in those ten seconds. The radio said encouragingly: "You're coming up beautifully at fifty feet". Ted Adair saw the fluorescent marker flashing toward him and flicked his switches. Red light; green light; the despatchers heaved out the cans. Braced in his seat, hands gripping the control column Mike had a fleeting photographic picture of tents, dogs and men bent against the wind and then suddenly he hurtled into a white void of low mist.

One second he could see the horizon, next he had the terrible empty sensation of flying inside a ping-pong ball. Instinctively his eyes rushed to his artificial horizon — but it was too late.

With a juddering crunch the port wing tip dug into the snow and was ripped into a jagged, twisted mass. A shudder went right through the Hastings. Someone on the intercom shouted "Christ". Mike slammed the throttles closed and wrestled with the control wheel. Desperately he struggled to lift his damaged wing.

"If it hits the snow again", the thought flashed through his mind, "she'll cartwheel nose-to-wingtip and we'll be done for".

For perhaps five long seconds he managed to hold that wing up while beads of sweat gathered on his face. He had to use such force he *bent* the control column — but it saved the day. Before the tom wing could flick back onto the ground the aircraft had smacked onto the snow on its belly and was careering at 120 knots across the ice-cap, tearing up a huge cloud of snow and gouging a wide trench behind it.

For a mile and a half it skidded in a series of big ground loops and then as it began to run backwards, first the port outer engine and then the port inner were wrenched from their mountings and rolled away into the snow in a shower of spurting oil and broken pipes.

Mike, pressed against the back of his seat by the violent movement yelled "Cut everything!"

Adair pushed the four buttons to operate the Graviner fire extinguishers in the engines — in those that remained — and Mosley snapped off the fuel cocks. And then suddenly it was all over.

The aircraft came to the end of its slithering journey, the snow shower subsided and then for a brief second a deathly silence came down on everything. In the cockpit there was a wave of immeasurable relief, relief that by some miracle they should have survived a crash which a few seconds earlier they had all felt was "it" — the end of everything. But here they were in the middle of the ice plateau with — apart from one damaged wing — an intact aeroplane.

Ted Adair struggled out of his straps and yelled two words — "Get out!"

CHAPTER 7

WHEN the wing tip hit the snow a lot of startling things happened to the ten men behind the pilots. Reg Michie who had just crawled out of the nose was standing behind the pilots' seats looking ahead. He was flung violently backwards, collided with second navigator Les Richardson and fell heavily onto Master Engineer Dick Mosley who was safely strapped to his seat. Richardson was also strapped in but Michie struck him with such force his seat snapped clean off at the swivel mounting. Frank Burke who had just undone his straps to make an adjustment to his radio was thrown off his feet, his head cracked hard against the transmitter and he remembered no more.

Five of the six men down in the fuselage were hooked to the end of nylon static lines — in case they slipped out of the open door during supply-heaving. The only man without a safety line round his waist was Smokey Stover. One second he was walking up the fuselage toward the crew compartment, the next he was flying through the air in the opposite direction, colliding with a shower of heavy jerrycans. He struggled to his feet and was clawing the side of the fuselage for support when the aircraft belly-smacked onto the snow and once more he went hurtling up the full length of the fuselage getting severely clouted halfway by the jerrycans which were now flying back, and cracking himself against his companions who were performing uncontrolled contortions in mid-air, like marionettes, on the end of their static lines.

"Chiefy" Boyd felt himself floating in the air and then he was thrown against the toilet door at the rear. Major Barker-Simson was suddenly plucked off his feet, swung from one side of the fuselage to the other like a pendulum weight and deposited on the floor under a heap of cans. A second later the sturdy frame of Corporal Yates crashed onto him. Private Jones had been busy stacking a pile of jerrycans near the forward bulkhead; he was snatched off his feet, dashed against the cockpit door then spun about on the end of his cord like a yo-yo.

Corporal Fussey thought his last moment had come as he was lifted off his feet and soared clean out through the open door. The freezing slipstream slapped his face and he had a vivid picture of the snow rushing up to meet him; then he felt a painful jerk round his waist and the safety line held him, dangling upside down outside the aircraft. "Suddenly a thousand icy-cold needles hit me in the face and I felt a great wave of joy and relief sweep over me" — his face was dragging in the snow and after what seemed to him an eternity he realized that the snow was no longer moving and the aircraft had stopped.

Ted Adair need not have yelled "Get out". Every man knew that any second damaged fuel pipes might spread the Hastings' high octane petrol onto the still hot motors and set the aircraft ablaze. Everybody except Mike Clancy, Reg Michie and Les Richardson scrambled for the open door, leapt out onto the soft snow and stumbled away clear of the aircraft. For a horrible moment Mike thought he was trapped. His desperate efforts to hold the port wing up had twisted the aileron wheel onto his right thigh and it was jammed. He finally freed himself with a fierce heave, reached up and opened the escape hatch in the cockpit roof and hauled himself out onto the top of the aircraft. A few seconds later the two navigators disentangled themselves and dashed out through the rear door; they were the last to leave the aircraft.

Meanwhile Mike was sitting on the roof counting the crew, standing a few yards away, to satisfy himself everybody was out. At first he thought one man was missing; his tally was only eleven. It was only when he counted them for a second time that he realized that *he* was the twelfth man. Then he slid down the nose and made a quick inspection of the aircraft.

Incredible as it seemed, apart from the buckled port wingtip and the gaping cavities where the two port engines had been, Hastings 492 was virtually undamaged. In English drizzle, African sun and steaming Far East monsoon she had served the R.A.F. faithfully and now far from her old tropical routes she had made her last touch-down, 8,000 feet above sea level under a grey Arctic sky. Already the restless drifting snow of the cap was beginning to trickle over her.

Suddenly Mike noticed that the starboard inner engine was steaming. Immediately he thought: "The old girl's going to burn after all." He bawled to the others: "Get to Hell away from the aircraft" and they all staggered a few yards further away behind the tail. When Mike reached them he found eleven dazed men in a quietly murmuring group. From man to man he went taking each by the arm and asking the same question. "Are you all right?" Yes, apart from bruises and minor cuts they thought they were uninjured. Smokey grinned. "Do you always land the son-of-a-bitch like that, Mike?" he asked.

It was then that Mike noticed Frank Burke. He was lying in the snow on his back, his head covered in blood. For a moment he thought his signaller was dead. But then he saw that Burke's mouth was open and his breath was coming away in clouds of steam. Burke had taken a nasty crack on the head when he hit the radio; he was unconscious and his nose was broken.

Mike took another look at the steaming engine. It reeked strongly of petrol but after Mosley had squirted it with several fire extinguishers Mike decided that the immediate fire danger was over and that they could with reasonable care return to the fuselage. Ted Adair had ripped open a medical kit and was attending to Burke and now they picked the unconscious signaller up and gently carried him inside the fuselage and laid him on an open parachute.

It was only now that they began to appreciate how bitterly cold it was; in fact it was 3°F — 29 degrees below freezing. A chilling breeze was filling the air with wind-blown snow and as the cold began to seep through their outer parkas and flying clothing and the initial shock of the crash wore off, the twelve men realized for the first time that the battle for survival against this inescapable cold was not going to be easy. Textbooks on arctic survival tell crews forced down in the snow that the warmest place is in the snow itself — if necessary in holes sunk below the surface. The doctrine is sound. One of the biggest killers in conditions of extreme cold is the wind which so swiftly lowers a man's body temperature. In a small snow shelter he is insulated from the heat-sapping wind often far more effectively than inside a damaged fuselage whose metal is a dangerously cold conductor.

Mike Clancy, however, had been left with an intact fuselage. It had the makings of a far more comfortable survival nest than the huge hole they would have had to have carved out of the snow to accommodate twelve men. Besides there wasn't much daylight left and it would have been difficult caring for an injured man in a snow hole. So he decided they should live, at least for the time being, inside the Hastings.

Quickly they closed all the doors and escape hatches and set about tidying up the chaos that lay inside. From end to end the fuselage was littered with a jumbled confusion of jerry cans, heavy chains, clothing, thermos flasks, lunch boxes and broken wood. It looked as if a great sledgehammer had made several vicious swipes up and down the whole interior.

Mike looked at the round cold metal walls of the fuselage and shivered. "If we're going to live and keep living in this ice box, we'll have to insulate the whole darned outfit," he said. So they ripped open every unopened parachute they could find and rigged up three separate compartments lined with coloured parachute silk drapings and on the floor laid sound-proofing material stripped from the cockpit and sackfuls of wood shavings from the undropped supplies. Every man found himself a job. There was little said. They were all wondering the same thing — how soon could their wives and families know that they were all safe and alive.

Burke was beginning to stir. Ted Adair was doing an excellent bit of first aid on his face when he opened his eyes, and looked round surprised to see he was back in the aircraft. Mike went over and knelt beside him. Burke was a particular friend — back at Topcliffe they used to attend the same little Catholic Church in the camp; their religion gave them a special bond. And Burke, whom a few minutes earlier Mike had thought dead, was repeating. "I'm all right skipper, I'm all right." Mike said quietly: "I'm damn sorry this happened, Frank," but Burke cut him short — "Don't worry about me; what about the others." Mike said the others were uninjured and Burke lapsed into unconsciousness again.

There *were* other injuries, however. Cheerful, good-natured Smokey Stover was the first to suffer from the delayed effect of the crash. He was stretching up to fasten a parachute when suddenly he stiffened and couldn't lower his arms. And then in his soft drawl he said, "I dunno Mike, but I seem to have hurt my back, it's giving me a helluva pain."

They didn't know it then but the American had fractured two ribs and two vertebrae. Carefully they laid him down beside Burke in the tented compartment nearest the cockpit. And then Major Barker-Simson who had earlier dismissed an ankle pain as "it's only a sprain, chaps" suddenly sat down. "I'm afraid I can't walk," he said. "There's something definitely wrong with my ankle." It was broken. Now with a quarter of their number casualties, there could be no question of living anywhere but in the fuselage.

It was now 30 minutes since they had come down and Mike was beginning to wonder if Commander Simpson had seen the crash when Corporal Fussey who was outside shouted: "They're coming!" All the uninjured tumbled outside and peered where Fussey was excitedly pointing. But in every direction there was only snow, snow onto which cold grey mist hung in a hazy impenetrable curtain. "I'll swear I saw a man and dog team over there," Fussey said. Shielding their faces from the wind they looked until their eyes turned red and watery. And then out of the mist, a hundred yards away like some ghostly spectre, came eight huskies. They were hauling a swaying sledge. On the sledge a man crouched, cracking a long whip. Close behind came two figures on skis. The expedition had found them.

Not immediately had the men of Northice realized what had happened to Hastings 492. As the aircraft ran over the D.Z. for the last time they had been more interested in the falling jerrycans which they had wanted to recover before the cans were buried in the snow and lost.

Of the next few minutes Commander Simpson later reported: "A few moments later when I looked after the aircraft, it seemed to have disappeared into the mist. Then suddenly I saw an unfamiliar something about a mile away looming through the mist. Its outline was not at all clear, and for a minute its significance did not sink into my mind. Then suddenly the terrible realization swept over me. I ran to the tent and shouted to Taylor who was operating the radio inside: 'Ken, Ken are you in contact with the aircraft?' 'Yes,' he replied, 'I've just been talking to them.' 'But are you in contact NOW? Try again quickly.'

"He spoke into his microphone, but no reply came back. Angus Erskine, and Peter Taylor were nearby with a sledge, the mist lifted slightly and we could just make out the outline of a big aircraft. Angus whipped up his dogs, and we hurried towards it as fast as the snow would let us, not knowing what terrible scene we were going to find. As we came nearer we saw that mercifully, the outline was reasonably intact. Then suddenly we saw a sign of life. A man was silhouetted near the nose and shortly after a door opened and four or five men appeared. As we came up Mike Clancy stepped forward from the little group."

It was a dramatic encounter, that unscheduled reunion between the explorers and the Hastings men. And there was deep emotion on both sides. In the grey half-light of the approaching Greenland twilight the aircrew walked out past the long sweep of the wing that would never fly again and welcomed these brave men of the ice. It was a curious feeling for both parties coming face to face: to the Commander and his men their "guests" looked extraordinarily pale, clean and smooth-shaven, while their own appearance at first horrified the new arrivals. Weeks of living in sunshine and blizzard, unable to wash for the instant frostbite it would have caused, had turned their bearded faces brown, oily and grimy. From their nostrils hung clusters of icicles and in patches on their cheeks superficial and unavoidable frostbite had turned the skin a sallow yellow.

The Commander gripped Mike's arm in his gloved hands. He was clearly upset. "My God, Mike," he said, "is anybody hurt?" Mike told him none of the injuries was serious. "And," he added, "I'm terribly sorry we've dropped in like this at tea time without warning."

"It was a dreadful moment for us all," Commander Simpson said, "but merciful God, you're all safe. Is there anything we can do for you immediately?"

Mike asked if they could flash a signal to Thule and Air Ministry reporting the crash and reassuring families. They went inside the fuselage and Mike drafted a signal which Angus Erskine and Peter Taylor took back across the mile of wind-swept snow to the tents of Northice, now visible for the first time between patches of mist. From a small aerial slung between two upright skis the message went out from the centre of the ice-cap to Britannia Lake. Within a few hours news of the crash had reached London and Thule.

Inside the fuselage Commander Simpson and the Hastings men held a survival conference. It was a serious situation for the expedition leader. They had made the arduous journey to Northice travelling only with the barest equipment and rations necessary to sustain them until stores could be dropped to them in bulk. There was limited time in which to complete the drops before the Arctic winter and now half the air dropping force had descended into their midst with three injured men. Northice now had only one aircraft to bring in its eighty tons of stores and the added major responsibility of helping twelve men, largely ignorant of the lore of the ice-cap, keep alive until... until what?

There were three alternatives the Commander said. They could be rescued by air; they could sledge out to Britannia Lake and winter there; they could spend the winter where they were at Northice. At the last two suggestions there were looks of undisguised dismay from the men in the fuselage; few of them fancied cramped dark months on the ice-cap nor an enforced sojourn at Britannia Lake *plus* a 250-mile snow trudge.

On the first alternative, air rescue, nobody felt they were justified in hanging much hope. They knew that the U.S.A.F. had made many rescues in the frozen Arctic — and at least one in Greenland — with ski-wheel Dakotas, but getting a heavy aircraft with a load of survivors off the ice-cap at 8,000 feet was another story altogether. At 8,000 feet an aircraft operates at greatly reduced power and it seemed doubtful that the Americans at Thule would consider the risk of such an undertaking. But secretly everybody hoped they would try. Helicopter rescue was ruled out by the distance — 480 miles — from Thule.

If it was necessary to sledge out to Britannia Lake, Commander Simpson said they would have to leave in about three weeks, as soon as the ice station was built. The injured would travel by sledge and the others would have to get along on skis. Averaging about eighteen miles a day with the wind behind them they should reach the base camp in two weeks. After spending the winter there they could return to England by air or sea in the spring of 1953. The Commander looked dubiously at the clothing the Hastings men were wearing. "If we *did* take you out that way," he said, "we'd have to get you properly kitted out; they'd have to drop you extra gear."

For the twelve of them to winter on the ice-cap immediate requests would have to be signalled for extra huts of the expedition's special design. And they would need a big air drop of food and equipment. In the spring they would be driven to the coast by weasel.

The twelve men looked at one another glumly. Whatever became of them, they thought, it looked as if they were in for a damn cold few days, weeks or more probably months.

Before he left, Commander Simpson gave a few tips about the ice-cap way of life. Everybody not working, he said, should stay in their sleeping bags with windproof clothing removed. They should avoid perspiring while working as sweat invariably froze to the skin — a quick way of getting frostbite. They should avoid flesh contact with any cold surfaces; even a cold cup would freeze to the lips and tear a painful strip of skin away when it was removed. They should eat plenty of food always followed by exercise to help generate body heat. Those not adequately clad should put on any extra clothing available on a share-out basis, aiming to copy as far as possible the expedition's clothing style. In any case they would signal for more clothing and blankets to be dropped as soon as possible.

And then the Commander made a big decision. He said: "I think the wisest thing I can do now is to move my whole camp over here beside you. Although we're only a mile away it's all of an hours' sledge journey in this twenty-five knot wind. If we stay there it will mean a lot of time wasted trekking backwards and forwards every day. Besides now you've bequeathed us this big aeroplane we might just as well make use of it; it will make an excellent store-house." They would begin moving next day, he said. Then, pulling his big parka hood over his head, the expedition leader strapped on his skis and was gone.

Inside the fueslage everybody felt better for the Commander's visit. He and his team had left behind some of the cheerfulness and confidence which radiated from them. Mike now set about organizing sub-zero fuselage life. Although not the senior officer he assumed leadership as Major Barker-Simson was incapacitated and looked like being confined to his sleeping bag. Ted Adair became deputy survival commander with the job of "medical supervisor" and official log writer.

Navigators Reg Michie and Les Richardson — or "Richie" as he was better known — were to be responsible for preparing every possible method of signalling and laying out recognition panels on the snow as well as establishing as soon as possible the *exact* position of the Hastings. "Chiefy" Boyd and Private Jones were appointed cooks and Corporal Fussey "official photographer" — his Army camera had been smashed in the crash but his own private camera was fortunately in one piece.

Although he couldn't forget the 1,000 gallons of inflammable fuel which still remained in the tanks Mike decided that in the rear of the fuselage at least, it was safe enough to have a couple of primuses burning continuously to get a little basic warmth into their cold metal shell. But to play safe he drew up a night watch rosta of four two-hour periods during each of which two men would be on duty.

By dusk the three fuselage tent compartments were completed. The biggest one next to the cockpit became the sick bay and general sleeping quarters. At the forward end the three injured men were laid in their sleeping bags but so they wouldn't block the cockpit door a narrow tented alleyway was left down the side. The second "tent room", which was made deliberately small, became a general ante-room, and dining-hall; the two primuses were kept burning here and it soon became known at the "fug hole". The third compartment became a kitchen, and food and equipment store.

The aircraft's survival crates had been undamaged in the crash and now the crew eagerly set about investigating the immediate usefulness of their contents. For hundreds of trips they had regarded these boxes rather as the pilot regards his parachute — as a necessary encumbrance which he is sure *he* will never need. Now at last the survival gear was coming into its own. It yielded sleeping-bags, cooking equipment, primus stoves, digging tools, arctic lanterns, cans of paraffin and methylated spirits and hard rations. When they had collected every scrap of food — including the emergency supplies in the aircraft's dinghies Mike reckoned that they had enough for sixteen days' careful eating or, if they rationed themselves strictly, for perhaps twenty days.

Presently "Chiefy" Boyd had a can of tea brewed. Sharing the cups and dipping them first into boiling water to prevent lip frostbite they all sat round the primuses in the "fug hole" — except the three injured men who lay silently side by side in their sleeping-bags like three cocoons.

Suddenly the door opened and a heavily built man with a big kindly-looking face stepped in out of the snow belching clouds of steam as he breathed. It was Graham Rollitt. He stood inside the door and looked around. Like the others his beard was matted with ice and his cheeks yellow with frostbite patches.

"Chaps," he said in his quiet deep voice, "I'm dreadfully sorry about this." From bulging pockets he produced a pile of tea, sugar, sweets and tobacco which he laid almost reverently down on a box. It was a gesture which touched every man in the fuselage.

Soon after Rollitt had left on his long ski drag back to the tents a mile to the north-east the cooks served up their first ice-cap meal — hot tinned stew and biscuits. It was a meal that was to become all too familiar during their stay at Northice. Everybody ate out of mess tins and because water froze immediately it touched the metal they "washed up" merely by scraping the tins. And then as it was too cold to do anything else everybody climbed into their sleeping-bags leaving Mike and Mosley to do the first fire watch.

Soon, when Mike peeped through the drapings into the sleeping compartment all he could see of his companions were ten sleeping-bags huddled together in a row for mutual warmth and above each bag a small spiral of steam. Only one face showed out of its bag and it gave Mike a friendly wink. It was Smokey.

Outside the wind whistled eerily round the Hastings and from time to time the buckled port wing creaked metallically. Wind-blown snow sifted over the wings with a hissing noise and inside it became bitterly cold. There was no escape from the cold; it seeped in everywhere, dry, biting cold which poured swiftly through the thickest clothing until the very bones ached with it. It came in through the tiniest cracks, through the doors, through the windows, but fiercest of all it welled up through the floor, the thin metal floor which lay hard on 8,500 feet of solid ice.

Mike and Mosley sitting by the spluttering primuses in the glow of the Arctic lantern they had suspended from the roof noticed that a layer of hoar frost was growing, thick and white on the fuselage walls behind the parachute drapings. Rubbing the frost off the window Mike peered out into the night. A long way away, across the ice he could see a light moving.

Someone at Northice was still up. "At least we have neighbours," he said.

At 2 a.m. Ted Adair and Corporal Yates came on watch and Mike and Mosley quickly slid into the sleeping-bags they had made warm. But it was too cold for more than fitful sleep. On all sides the sleeping-bags were heaving and flexing as the sleepless occupants, grunting and muttering about the flickering cold tried to find a position more comfortable and possibly warmer than the last. It was a miserable night and nobody was sorry when cold fingers of light heralded their first ice-cap dawn.

Mike struggled out of his bag and tried to beat some warmth into his numbed body. He looked around him. What a bleak scene it was. Even in the half light he could see the icicles hanging in thin cold needles from the roof and the frost sparkling on the parachute drapings. A row of bleary faces looked out of their bags miserably, faces that were showing their first smudge of stubble, stubble already sprinkled with crystals of hoar frost. The three injured men looked specially dejected.

Frank Burke had now regained consciousness but his concussion was giving him a continuous blinding headache. He smiled weakly at Mike. Smokey's back was giving him excruciating pain. He hadn't eaten since the crash and there was no position in which he could effectively relieve the agony in his spine. He lay there thinking of his pretty wife, Marjorie, in Portland, Maine, wondering if she knew of the crash and that he was alive. He called to Mike to fetch him the invalids' jerrycan. "A shame it is you have to lose that good heat," Mike said when Smokey handed it back to him.

Reg Michie and Corporal Fussey were now on watch. Crouched over the primuses they were sipping tea. Mike forced open the door which had frozen during the night and jumped out onto the snow. It was a clear grey morning and, he was surprised to discover, not as cold as the previous day. Actually the ice-cap was experiencing one of its periodic "heat waves" and during the day the temperature was to rise even further to 46°F — 14 degrees *above* freezing. Mike walked slowly round the aircraft and marvelled again that it had survived the crash so well; he felt exceedingly grateful to Handly Page for making such a sturdy aeroplane. During the night the wind had drifted snow against the fuselage; already it was banked nearly three feet high and he realized that it would only be a matter of time before the aircraft was completely buried. Already the big trench which the Hastings had sliced out of the snow on its long slide had disappeared. Over on the horizon he could see the two tiny pyramids of the expedition's tents. Away to the west it was still dark. Somewhere over there, he thought, was Thule; already men would be astir in their warm quarters, sitting down to ample American breakfasts. Mike shivered and went back into the fuselage.

Down in the sleeping compartment there was a bedlam of noise. Men were shouting, laughing and singing. "What the devil's this in aid of" said Mike, who could see little in their situation to celebrate. But when he thrust aside the drapings he saw that they were wishing Smokey many happy returns of the day. "Happy birthday dear Smokey, happy birthday to you", they sang. The American who was thirty-five had casually mentioned the fact the day before; somebody had remembered it. He lay in his sleeping-bag his whiskered face grinning to hide the pain he felt.

After that the cooks served breakfast — sausage, bacon, stew, hard bread and tea — and everybody except the injured climbed out to face their first full ice-cap day. Outside the sudden rise in temperature had brought a low overcast over the cap and it looked unlikely that any aircraft from Thule would risk a supply drop in such poor visibility.

Presently there were shouts and the yap of dogs outside; the expedition had begun to move camp and had arrived with their first sledge load. Commander Simpson came breezily into the Hastings. "How's everything this morning; what sort of a night did you have?" he asked. Then like a house surgeon on his morning round of a hospital ward the Commander went over to the injured. Gently he examined Burke's head. "Only a slight dent" he said, "nothing serious". He began to tell the three men then of his plans for sledging them out to Britannia Lake but Smokey interrupted — "Heck Commander," he said. "I sure appreciate your concern for us but honestly the way I feel now I reckon that unless I get out of here by air I shan't go out at all. I just wouldn't survive the sledge journey and six months at your base camp." Smokey said he was darn sure his people would attempt an air rescue; it was that or an ice-cap grave for him.

During the night a signal had come in from Air Ministry requesting details of the crash with which to forewarn pilots making future low runs over Northice. Mike drafted a reply in which he described his "white-out".

The term was a relative stranger in the R.A.F.'s physiological terminology which already included the familiar descriptions black-out, grey-out and red-out. It was, however, well known to experienced Arctic pilots of the U.S.A.F. In fact not long before an American pilot flying over snow country suddenly felt his aircraft hit the ground. Instantly he applied full power and was able to climb away. He had no idea he was anywhere near the snow. "White-out" had deceived him. On another occasion a U.S.A.F. pilot was flying a Dakota between two bases in Greenland. Unforecasted winds blew him a few miles off course, and over the inland ice. He was — or so be thought — flying in visual contact with the ground. But suddenly from cruising peacefully along at 125 knots the crew felt a shudder, the aircraft slithered a few yards and they came to an abrupt halt on the snow. They had flown straight onto the gently upward sloping ice-cap. The pilot had lost his natural horizon when sky and snow merged in one white blur and for the last few seconds before his unintentional landing he had been flying in a "white-out".

There are several forms of this insidious peril to snow flying whose most dangerous feature is its tendency to be absent one moment and there the next. One of the chief causes is the weakening of the sun's rays in their long journey to the Arctic through the earth's atmosphere and the diffusion of this scattered light still further often by the tiny crystals of ice haze. The pilot's immediate remedy when these conditions blot out the horizon with which he is keeping his aircraft on an even keel is to switch his attention to his flight instruments and to get a true indication of his attitude from them. The greatest danger from "white-out" is near the ground for there in the short space of time between the pilot realizing his horizon has disappeared and his switch to instruments he can be bouncing on the snow. In the worst conditions of "white-out" even men and dogs on the snow can lose their visual horizon; they have difficulty in walking upright and constantly fall over the smallest snowdrift in their way.

Ten years earlier another aircraft had crashed on the Greenland ice-cap in very similar circumstances but with a more tragic outcome. It was a Flying Fortress of the American Air Transport Command being ferried from America to Europe. On November 9, 1942 it crashed near the edge of the cap in south-east Greenland; like Hastings 492 its port wing tip had struck the snow. In "white-out" conditions — "flying in milk" he called it, the pilot had believed he was much higher than in fact he was. The Fortress slid 200 yards on its belly and its fuselage broke in two. It had nine men aboard and it was five months before the last of the survivors were rescued.

Close to the coast they were in a badly crevassed region of the cap; in fact the wrecked Fortress was completely surrounded by crevasses. Despite this and despite atrocious winter weather a Coastguard Grumman amphibian landed *wheels down* and took off two of the men. It was flying out later with another man when it crashed killing all aboard.

Two rescuers eventually reached the Fortress from the coast with propeller-driven sleds. Less than 100 yards from the aircraft one of them disappeared for ever, sled and all, into a huge crevasse. The other sled taking three men — one of them seriously frostbitten — out to the coast, broke down and the sled party minus one man who dropped into a crevasse spent from November to March sheltering from almost continuous blizzards in a snow hole dug in the ice — only a few miles from the aircraft where the remaining three members of the crew were also huddled in a snow house. Five months after the Fortress crashed, both marooned parties were taken off by a Catalina flying-boat which landed on the cap on its hull — the first time that a flying-boat had been deliberately put down on the icecap this way.

As the expedition's radio was losing power through weak batteries — they were having trouble with their petrol driven generator — Commander Simpson asked if they could set up their equipment in the aircraft's cockpit: but Mike had to say no. He was still worried about the aircraft's fuel, the starboard inner engine was still fuming and having earlier disconnected their own radio batteries he didn't want to revive the risk of a radio spark igniting the whole aircraft. However he gave the Commander an R.A.F. emergency tent in which to run his generator outside and agreed to let Ken Taylor install his radio in a spare toilet compartment in the tail far away from the petrol tanks. Taylor rigged up an aerial between two skis dug into the snow.

Because the expedition now had the dual task of moving camp and collecting the dropped stores from the D.Z. Mike called for volunteers to help. He felt it was vital that they should get out of the unhealthy atmosphere of the fuselage and exercise.

Soon the lonely square mile of ice-cap containing the aircraft and the tents of Northice was a scene of feverish activity. A stream of dog, sled and man traffic began to furrow a deep track in the soft snow between the two points and slowly the black dots which represented uncollected loads all over the dropping zone were collected and stacked beside the Hastings. During the day those not helping the expedition, banked a huge pile of snow over the simmering engine, dug out frozen oil from the aircrafts sumps for use as a smoke signal, rigged up a snow melting tank over one of the primuses and added further to the interior lining of the fuselage.

Out in the freezing wind on the dropping zone the Hastings volunteers quickly realized that they had let themselves in for a bitter task. Unlike the explorers they were not dressed for the snow and the cold cut into them like a rapier; unlike the explorers they were unaccustomed to exertion at 8,000 feet above sea level and soon their hearts began to pound and their heads reeled dizzily. The only R.A.F. man who was really warm was Mike — but he was too warm. He experimented with one of the aircraft's survival suits, a garment which he blew up round himself with air until he looked like a living advertisement for a well-known brand of tyre. The suit was so exhausting it took him a painful hour to reach the dropping zone and he was too weak to work when he got there. He never used it again. In any case it was only meant for stationary survival.

On the dropping zone the crew saw for the first time what became of the supplies they had pushed out from above. They were buried up to four feet in the snow; only the tips of some gave a clue that there was anything there at all. It was a back-breaking business digging them out with snow shovels and lumping them onto the sledges. And all the while the huskies who had not yet recovered from their wet sea voyage and the arduous journey from Britannia Lake fulfilled Commander Simpson's earlier prophesy by "howling and stinking". The smell was so nauseating that the Hastings men quickly learnt to remain upwind of them. On that first day they were howling with special feeling because one of their colleagues who had died during the night had been taken away from them before they could make a meal of him. The dead husky lay under a tarpaulin and the others knew it.

There was no sentiment among these perpetually ravenous dogs. If one became weaker than the others he stood in peril of being killed and eaten; every morning the Commander counted his teams in case the tally was less than the day before. Constantly fighting, snarling and entangling their traces the dogs would devour anything containing the faintest suspicion of nourishment that came their way; one dog's excreta was immediately eaten by another because its owner knew instinctively that *his* system could extract no further good from it. Human excreta was an even greater prize.

But for all their savage instincts the dogs remained a constant source of fascination to the Hastings men. Without them Northice would never have been established. On a flat surface in good snow conditions a ten or twelve dog team could haul a load of nearly half a ton forty miles a day. Each team had its leader, known as the King dog, which regularly demonstrated its authority by fighting every other dog in the pack. On the trail the leader always knew immediately which dogs weren't pulling their full share and would swing round to deliver the slackers a sharp bite on the hind leg. At Northice they slept in the snow, curled up in furry balls their heads buried in their paws. Often in the morning, drifting snow would have covered them but snow was only another blanket for the Greenland husky. Unlike their masters they were only uncomfortable when the temperature climbed *above* freezing.

That afternoon the explorer's tents were brought over and set up close by the Hastings. The R.A.F. and the British North Greenland Expedition were now one consolidated enterprise, eighteen men strong. A stream of radio messages began to pass to and from Britannia Lake but the base camp operator was not always immediately able to relay signals to Thule and London. For hours on end the Arctic atmospherics would black-out all Britannia Lake's long-range transmission and reception making it necessary for signals to be relayed from station to station all the way down the east coast to the southern tip of Greenland and then by similar stages up the west coast to Thule — a roundabout journey of nearly 2,500 miles as against 800 miles straight across the cap. The expedition's doctor at Britannia Lake gave radio advice to help diagnose and treat the injuries and a Thule message said that no aircraft would be flying out that day owing to bad weather on the west coast. Later another signal from Thule brought the cheerful news that a rescue aircraft would attempt to land at Northice at the earliest opportunity. A wave of excitement swept through the fuselage at this and for the rest of the evening long speculative discussions ensued on the prospects of success of such an operation.

Although the twelve men didn't know it they were now a centre of worldwide interest. Edition by edition London's newspapers were describing their plight, press cables were carrying the news to overseas papers and they now had a regular place in every B.B.C. bulletin. Throughout England the novelty of the "men on the ice-cap" had become a prominent topic of conversation and for some people the little drama in Greenland soon acquired the interest of a Test Match.

At R.A.F. Station Topcliffe telephones rang incessantly; some people wanted news, others had arctic survival advice to offer and a few enthusiasts volunteered their personal services in any rescue attempt. Every mail brought further offers, more advice, and even gifts to be dropped to the stranded crew. From nearby Harrogate a man wrote to give the R.A.F. the benefit of his Yorkshire snow experience. "In the past", he wrote, "I did some skiing over our Yorkshire hills, so I thought it might be advisable to let you know some of the experiences as they might be found helpful if your crew of the Hastings aircraft find they have to march or ski some hundreds of miles. When I was fit I found I could do about twenty-five miles a day. Once I had to spend a night out so rolled large snow balls and built them up into a small tunnel-shaped hut, crawled in, built up the entrance with two large snowballs and laid down on my skis turned upside down for insulation purposes and slept like a log until eleven a.m. next morning. In Greenland I should think the snow would not be in condition for rolling and would have to be cut ... If your people in Greenland are not used to skiing I don't expect they would do twenty-five miles a day; ten miles would be quite enough to give them at first.

"I think it might be possible to make a double skin tent which could be blown up like a rubber dinghy; this air between the skins would insulate from the cold". In a postscript the writer added: "Racing at high speed down slopes should be banned except for the very expert who can do all the swings perfectly because even a broken ankle would be a serious disaster which could quite easily lead to death of one or more of a party. Besides it is often difficult to see what the hill below is like and one might easily take off over a cliff cither of rock or ice".

Topcliffe's Flying Wing Adjutant Richard Harben replied that this advice would certainly be conveyed to the men on the ice-cap "who will, I know, be touched at this expression of your personal interest in their welfare".

Meanwhile high-level discussions had begun between Air Ministry and the U.S.A.F. over plans for rescue and already aircraft of the American No 6 Air Rescue Squadron were converging on Thule. At that time the squadron had no aircraft permanently based at Thule; its nearest flight was at Bluie West 1, 1,200 miles to the south. But immediately the squadron had been alerted it threw all its available resources of men and aircraft into the rescue operation. Not only from southern Greenland but from Goose Bay in Labrador and Fort Pepperell in Newfoundland, 2,000 miles away, No 6 Squadron's aircraft and crews, specially trained in snow landings, were alerted and sent hurrying to Thule. They included a twin-engined Grumman Albatross amphibian and a ski-wheeled Dakota both equipped with JATO — jet assisted take-off installations. Unfortunately the Dakota, on which the greatest hopes for a successful landing at Northice were pinned, was delayed in its dash to Thule. Half-way, at Bluie West 8, it developed mechanical trouble; then it was grounded by bad weather.

At Thule the same low cloud and high winds were preventing David Wright in Hastings 490 from flying to Northice. The aircraft's load had been rearranged to include nearly a ton of emergency supplies for the marooned party — extra clothing and blankets, fresh food, cigarettes, chocolate, whisky, beer and meat scrounged from the mess kitchens at Thule for the huskies.

Out at Northice the twelve men were settling down inside the derelict fuselage for their second night. A few yards away their "hosts" were crawling into the far warmer haven of their tents — Commander Simpson, Richard Hamilton and Angus Erskine into one, Graham Rollitt and the two Taylors into the other. During the night the temperature began to drop. It went down to — 5°F — 37 below. It was a foretaste of even more bitter cold to come.

CHAPTER 8

NEXT morning, September 18, the fuselage men opened bleary eyes to the tune of a high-pitched medley of static and signals from the rear toilet compartment. Ken Taylor was already in touch with Britannia Lake sending out the central Greenland weather report. Soon he poked his bearded face out of the door and called up the fuselage: "Wake up lads, there's news from Thule for you. They say an aircraft's on the way."

The news electrified the fuselage into boisterous activity. In a flash the sleepless night, the aching inescapable cold, the frost which clung to everything and the dawn depression were forgotten. An aircraft could mean rescue. Why, perhaps in a few hours they would be soaking themselves in steaming Thule baths.

Mike ordered every able-bodied man outside to mount a 360° watch in case they could see the aircraft before it spotted the camp. Despite the crisp blue morning, ice haze cut the visibility to a few miles. The aircraft was a long time coming and then around midday came a big disappointment. Ken Taylor shouted from the radio that it was not a rescue plane; it was the other Hastings.

Presently they could hear the faint throb of its engines somewhere in the haze; it was impossible to tell from which direction it was approaching. Then Mike spotted its shadowy outline away to the south. He yelled back to Taylor inside the aircraft: "Tell him to turn port, port". Somebody set fire to the frozen oil they had dug out of the sumps to make a smoke signal but in the frigid air of the cap it sent up a white instead of a black cloud. But the smoke wasn't necessary. The pilot,

Ian Iddison, had turned left and soon his signaller, Sergeant Bowler, said on the radio that they could see Northice. Taylor turned up the volume and they could all hear Bowler's cheery voice saying that they were going to drop medical supplies and clothing then more stores for the expedition. Mike was relieved to hear this; he didn't want their own demands to interfere with the dropping of the Commander's equally essential supplies.

The Hastings roared over at 600 feet. From its open door tiny figures waved to them and "Scoop" Finbow took pictures which a few days later were to be prominently featured on the front page of London's evening papers. And then an American voice crackled out of Taylor's radio. It was Captain Oswald Wetzel, Thule's provost marshal, an old friend of Smokey's.

"Smokey boy, this is Wetzel up here," he called. "How the hell did you get yourself into that situation?" Ken Taylor obligingly relayed the message through the clutter of parachute drapings to the other end of the fuselage where Smokey lay in his sleeping-bag and the American shouted back: "It's all right for you Wetzel up there, *you're* warm." He joked but inwardly he was depressed and lonely.

Captain Wetzel was still talking. He was giving them details of plans to rescue them by air within the next two days. Either a Dakota or a Grumman amphibian would attempt a landing and Thule wanted a report as soon as possible on the suitability of the snow surface. Then an English voice came on the radio. It was Squadron Leader Hassan, an R.A.F. medical officer aboard the Hastings who had been passing through Thule in the celebrated long-range Lincoln *Aries* from Manby. Now he was making a gallant offer to parachute down if necessary to attend to the three injured men. Asking him to "standby" Mike hurried over to Commander Simpson to get his views. But the

Commander said he didn't think any of the injuries were serious enough to warrant this splendid gesture.

So they thanked the medico who gave them further advice to help Ted Adair in his treatment of the patients. When the injuries were described to him Hassan asked Ted to examine Smokey, feel certain parts of his back and note his reactions. When Ted had done this the doctor said he should treat the injury as a spinal one adding that he would have a Stokes stretcher dropped in which Smokey could be fastened and made more comfortable. Frank Burke should be kept in his sleeping-bag and on no account allowed to get up; the Major's ankle should be regarded as fractured and bandaged accordingly.

While this air-to-ground medical consultation was continuing the Hastings was circling and dropping supplies on the new D.Z. which had been marked out 200 yards behind the aircraft. The big bulk of the crashed aircraft with its red markings was an invaluable aid to Ian Iddison's height judging and Mike was able to offer him further assistance for his difficult low runs by radioing up an accurate pressure setting for his sensitive altimeter from his own instrument — it fluctuated with changes in pressure over the ice-cap around the 8,400 feet mark; never again would its hands slowly unwind to near-sea-level readings.

Again and again the Hastings swept in over Northice leaving behind it a multi-coloured cluster of parachutes drifting sedately down, an incongruous spectacle in this hazy white world. Shielding his face with gloved hands against the wind that burned cold on his cheeks Mike looked wistfully up at the circling aircraft. The whole unreality of his situation was brought home to him by the sight of that Hastings on whose wings the Arctic sun was now glinting palely. He wasn't used to looking at things from below; his place was up there and he badly wanted to be back there.

Now the Hastings was making its low run for the free drops. It roared in at 100 feet, engines whining; out flew the brown bundles and on the snow little white puffs burst into the air. Then the whine took on a sudden deeper note as the aircraft climbed away, leaving a long low condensation trail hanging in a tubular cloud over the dropping zone. The cloud was still there when they came round again. Mike shouted to Ken Taylor to warn Ian Iddison and a little later Taylor shouted from the fuselage: "They've just had a white-out!" But Iddison at 100 feet had quickly gone over to his instruments and climbed away. By the time he came in again the contrail cloud had blown off the D.Z.

The drop took the Hastings an hour and a quarter. When the last load had come down and Bowler had asked "Is there anything we can bring you tomorrow?" the aircraft pointed its nose to the west and headed away to Thule.

Out on the dropping zone the Commander and his men were busy collecting the loads on sledges. Everything was accounted for except a big Herman-Nelson petrol heater which was supposed to have been dropped. As the temperature was still falling this was a big disappointment to the fuselage men. But there were compensations in a big bundle of extra sleeping-bags, clothing, blankets and most welcome of all Mukluk boots. There was a special package for Smokey. It contained a bottle of whisky from his fellow-officers at Thule and, to his delight, a letter from his wife. The letter was a week old, and had been written before the crash and told Smokey that his fifteen-year-old son had been running with his high school's cross country team to strengthen his legs for basketball. The letter took Smokey's mind off his own misfortune and for a long time he lay there with his thoughts back in the green countryside of Maine. The voice of Ted Adair brought him back to reality. "Smokey old boy," he was saying, "we've had medical advice on your back and have been advised to strap it up with adhesive plaster."

Smokey shuddered at the thought of such an operation but just the same he joked: "Okay doc, whatever you say."

To raise the temperature in the sick bay they concentrated all the lamps in that part of the fuselage and when the temperature had crept from 40° to a mere 10° below freezing Ted and Mike gently eased Smokey out of his sleeping-bag. While several of the crew supported him Ted quickly stripped off his four layers of clothing. The American gritted his teeth; every movement was agony and his bare back went so blue with cold the men around him had to rub the circulation back into it. Quickly Ted strapped on the plaster and in less than a quarter of an hour Smokey was back in his bag. For the first time since the crash Ted gave him morphine that night. And to help him sleep he gave Frank Burke codeine. Soon the two worst casualties were sleeping for the first time in three days, although for Smokey it was half sleep half delirium. During the night he began to talk with great feeling to an imaginary crew of an aircraft of which he was pilot. Major Barker-Simson woke suddenly to hear him giving lifelike orders and calling up a control tower for landing instructions. Then he lapsed into restless sleep again.

Members of the expedition, too, took advantage of Ted's expanding medical locker and several of them came in for first aid for cut and tom hands.

That night, their third on the ice-cap, was their first really cheerful one. The temperature dropped to 40° below freezing and away from the two primuses the frost began to form again thick and white. The outer canvas covers of the sleeping-bags became too cold to touch with bare hands and the inner cotton sheet froze board stiff. To overcome this they discarded the covers and wrapped the kapok inner bag in four or five blankets. This way everybody got a few hours' sleep.

The fourth day was the coldest yet. And when Commander Simpson breezed into the fuselage with long icicles hanging from his nostrils and his beard stiff with frost to announce cheerily "How's everybody this morning; the temperature outside is minus twenty-five degrees" nobody felt like leaving their sleeping-bags. But when the Commander announced that Thule had radioed that a definite rescue attempt had now been decided on, rows of bearded faces popped out of the long line of frosty sleeping-bags. And then the Commander asked Mike "What are the chances of getting a working party from here this morning?"

Mike said: "Sure we'll be after helping you" but he knew in his heart that digging supplies out of the frozen snow had long ago lost any little appeal it ever had as a diversion from the monotony of fuselage life. When the Commander had gone there were load groans from the sleeping-bags and muttered anonymous comments of "Slave driver" and "If I have to go out there again I'm sure I'll die".

Soon, however, the delicious aroma of cooking bacon began to filter through the drapings from the kitchen and presently "Chiefy" Boyd's black bearded face poked through to announce "Breakfast's ready". Within a few minutes there were nine empty sleeping-bags and everybody was enjoying their best breakfast since leaving Thule. The previous day's drop had added tinned bacon, puffed wheat and fresh-baked bread to the menu. There was now temporarily revived enthusiasm for the working party and soon the volunteers were out in the snow searching for missing supplies, digging them out and loading the sledges. And later when they returned to the fuselage warm from work they knew that despite the temptations of the "fug hole" it was to their own physical advantage to force themselves to take this exercise. For now the effects of the enforced unhealthy life of the fuselage, the continuous nagging cold, lack of sleep and altitude lassitude were beginning to undermine the health of most of them. They were developing hacking chest colds which grew daily worse, some were suffering badly from indigestion and to Smokey's already considerable sufferings was added a touch of pneumonia.

They hadn't washed or shaved for four days, their bodies were grimed and oily from the lantern and primus fumes, their clothes were stiff with dirt, their beards were constantly matted with ice and their noses sore from rubbing off nostril icicles. The only steps toward personal hygiene they could safely take were hot water mouth rinses and rotation of clothing. When the garment next to the skin became grubby or damp it was pushed back in the "queue" and the next outer layer moved in. But soon even this had little value for every garment was equally dirty.

Out on the D.Z. the snow was littered with equipment; red, orange and green parachutes lay everywhere. The Commander was anxious to get it collected before the next drop. He didn't want more loads crashing onto those already on the snow. As it was some of the parachutes had failed to open and several plywood hut sections were damaged.

Already Graham Rollitt was digging a deep twenty-foot square hole in the snow in which to build the hut. He cut the snow out in big blocks which were stacked round the edge to make a protecting wall. Mike and Corporal Fussey joined him in the hole. Here there was partial escape from the wind which blew in an incessant numbing blast. The Commander had given the hut a high priority. As soon as it was finished he had suggested that the casualties be moved into it, for it would be far warmer than the metal fuselage.

During the day Mike made another inspection of the starboard inner engine. It had now stopped fuming and as the fire danger now seemed much reduced he told Commander Simpson he thought it safe enough to operate the expedition's radio and generator from the crew compartment. Ken Taylor immediately rigged his set up in the new position and cut a hole in the fuselage to run out the exhaust from his petrol generator. The radio was now close to the sick-bay and the sound of voices coming in clearly from Britannia Lake helped to pass the dreary day for the patients.

Ken Taylor spent most of his time working on his radio. He worked two daily schedules with Britannia Lake at seven a.m. and eight p.m. Because much of his work required delicate finger adjustments he worked without gloves more than any of the others and frostbite had badly blistered his hands. But he was cheerfully unperturbed and when Smokey drew attention to the bulging blisters he dismissed it with: "Nothing to worry about, it's only the skin. Besides I can still work the key with my knuckles."

Among the stores from the previous day's drop several crates of clothes were found far out on the D.Z. almost completely buried in the snow. Eagerly the Hastings men sledged them back to the fuselage and the boxes were forced open. As the contents were hauled out there were incredulous groans. The R.A.F. men's dressing gowns, thin socks, bedroom slippers and cotton shirts complete with cuff links and studs had been sent out. Apparently someone at Thule had paid a quick visit to their rooms and gathered up all the clothes they could find. It was as well that they could not hear the yells of mirth with which this useless clothing was greeted. Fortunately there were compensations in a handsome pile of thick woollen clothing; soon everybody wore extra underclothing, several pairs of thick socks and up to four sweaters.

Again bad weather prevented an air drop. Conditions at Northice deteriorated during the day and by mid-afternoon the cold had forced all the store collectors back into the fuselage. The wind now howled round the aircraft with a fury they had not so far experienced and with it came stinging showers of loose snow. Several of the crew had narrow escapes from frostbite and only just reached the warmth of the "fug hole" before all feeling left their feet, hands or faces.

With the temperature now down to 50° below — and still dropping — the "fug hole" was fast becoming the only spot at Northice where they could keep any circulation in their grimy limbs. Mike had now permitted smoking and the "fug hole" with its garish coloured drapings had all the atmosphere of a smoky night-club. Bored and weary, the grisled inhabitants huddled together in the pale light of the storm lantern discussing again and again their prospects of rescue. They had begun to exhaust all the stories they knew, had read the few tattered magazines they had and didn't dare risk removing their gloves to play cards. Outside the wind moaned monotonously and occasionally the howl of a husky or a shouted oath told them that despite bitter cold and wind the six men of the expedition were still hard at work.

That evening the radio brought more news of rescue. When the squeals and distorted voices from his set had finally died away Ken Taylor came down the fuselage to share their meal of biscuits, meat and vegetable. "Well chaps," he said with the infectious grin he always wore, "It won't be long now. The day after tomorrow they hope to get a Dak out and take some of you off. If that's successful the aircraft will return the following day for the rest." A cheer greeted this news but when Taylor added that the rescuers had also requested an ambitious runway half a mile long the smiles quickly disappeared. Somebody said: "Hell we're not a private construction company".

Thule had asked for a carefully marked out runway into wind, smoke pots to indicate wind direction and requested that a sledge be driven down the runway when the aircraft was overhead to show the pilot which way he should land. Ted Adair summed up their feelings about the runway in the log that night. "It will be done", he wrote, "but it's not quite as simple a job to do here as it must appear at Thule. Many of the crew have severe chest colds which make work at this altitude and temperature very exhausting".

Saturday, September 20 was their fifth day on the ice-cap and the coldest they had so far experienced. When the Commander came in to pay his early morning respects he announced that the outside temperature was minus twenty-nine degrees. "Blimey" said one of the Army men with awe, "sixty below". In the fuselage the further temperature drop was all too apparent. The cold bit through the floor, through all the sacks of wood shavings with which they had carpeted it, through the blankets, sleeping-bags, and layers of clothes into every man's bones. The parachute drapings gleamed white with hoar frost and the rows of stiff sleeping-bags crackled as their occupants turned in desperate warmth-seeking contortions. Somebody who had foolishly picked up a mess tin flung it aside with a yell. It took a long strip of his skin with it and was a painful lesson to the others to keep bare hands away from metal objects at sixty below.

This morning the cooks, Boyd and Jones, made a gallant gesture and served breakfast in bed. It had to be eaten immediately it left the primuses or it was too cold for the lips; tea, even after the cups had been dipped in boiling water had ice floating on it within three minutes of pouring.

Out in the snow where the air was so cold it seemed to burn the lungs, Mike organized a runway construction party. Earlier he had had a discussion with Smokey about the runway requirements for a ski-wheeled Dakota. Smokey, who had himself landed ski-wheeled Dakotas both in Alaska and at Nord weather station in Independence Fiord in the far north of Greenland, told him that from what he had seen of the snow at Northice it looked suitable. He warned Mike to point the runway down the furrows of the *sastrugi* but said that there was no need to attempt to level out these six to twelve-inch high snow ridges, the ice-cap's only extrusion which lay four to five feet apart. "The chances are Mike," Smokey had said, "that they will land an S.A.16."

"What the hell's an S.A.16" asked Mike. The letters and numbers with which the Americans named their aircraft often completely cloaked their identity for the R.A.F.

"It's a little twin-engined ship — a Grumman Albatross amphibian."

"Amphibian?" said Mike incredulously. "How could you be landing an amphibian on snow?"

Smokey said: "Yeah, sure you can. The hull just sinks into the snow, just like on water, and little extension skis on the floats keep the floats from digging into the snow."

It sounded cockeyed and thoroughly improbable to Mike. He didn't say so to Smokey but he decided he would believe such a landing when he saw it.

Throughout that bitter fifth day the rescue runway took shape. They laid it into wind from east to west, 300 yards behind the Hastings which had come to rest pointing at the North Pole. Dr Hamilton went out with them with a dog team and a sledge load of coloured parachutes. Mike and Dick Mosley walked ahead of the sledge pacing out fifty yard intervals at each of which they laid out a chute and anchored it with snow blocks. Holding gloved hands over their faces and sometimes walking backwards to protect their cheeks from the wind they laid a 600-yard long row of markers. Then they came back repeating the performance fifty yards to one side. The rescue pilot now had two rows of coloured objects between which to land and keep his aircraft straight at the critical moment of his touch-down. At the down-wind end of the runway they laid a large fluorescent panel in the shape of a T to give the pilot his landing direction and marked the touchdown point with two big pyramids of coloured parachutes. Beside these they laid a broken engine cowling filled with a frozen solid black lump of oil, another wind indicator — if the pilot could see its white smoke against the snow. Just in case he couldn't Mike decided that when the aircraft arrived overhead he would set fire to one of the big Hercules engines which had broken away during their snow slide and which now lay several hundred yards from the Hastings half buried in the creeping snow. To this end they put a tin of petrol in readiness beside the engine. And finally they climbed onto the wings of the aircraft and brushed the wind-blown snow off the red Arctic markings. Every assistance they could give their rescuers in finding the lonely little camp and landing safely was worthwhile.

Late that afternoon David Wright's Hastings came out from Thule and made a further supply drop. But it was so fiercely cold outside that none of the fuselage men were very interested in the now familiar spectacle of parachute loads coming down. Their only interest was in the Herman-Nelson heater which they had been promised and with which they hoped to transform their fuselage ice-box into a more habitable place. This time the heater did arrive.

It was a big sturdy-looking piece of equipment and it took five men to dig it out of the snow into which it had become deeply embedded on landing. The R.A.F. men had never seen one before and at first were at a loss to know how to put its complicated machinery of fans and petrol burners into operation. By the time someone had discovered the book of instructions which had been dropped with it, it was too dark to do anything with it that day. Mosley was appointed O.C. heater and retired to the fug-hole to study the manual. Smokey said: "Once you get that thing going fellers you'll be able to run around this ship in your underwear!"

Among the expedition stores the Hastings had dropped was more food. Mike overheard Commander Simpson sledging in a load of flour, tinned meat and dehydrated vegetables say: "At least we can vary our old menu of pemmican and biscuits, biscuits and pemmican."

The obvious joy with which the explorers contemplated a little variety from the monotony of the sledge rations on which they had existed for weeks gave Mike an inspiration. Why not as a small gesture invite the expedition into the fuselage to share some of their own food? He hurried back to the "fughole" to sound the others. There was an immediate response. The cooks said they thought they could cope and Ted Adair agreed to make a small allocation from the few bottles of spirits he was holding against an emergency. Mike decided to hold the "dining-in night" that night. The explorers said they would be delighted to come. At what time should they arrive and what would they be expected to wear? Mike said seven o'clock and everything they could lay hands on.

It was a highly successful if unorthodox party in that lonely cold metal shell in the middle of the great ice-cap. The hosts tidied up the fuselage and rearranged the parachute drapings to make one big "dining hall" out of the sleeping-quarters and the "fug-hole". They hung two storm lanterns from the roof and spread sleeping-bags and blankets over the floor. Ted gently opened a whisky bottle and counted out eighteen paper cups. A stimulating aroma began to drift through from the kitchen where the tin opener was working overtime and the chefs were holding a secret and inaudible conference of their own.

Promptly at seven o'clock the six guests crawled out of their tents, wrestled with the aircraft's frozen door and slipped quickly inside. In the short time the door was open the inside temperature lost 10° of its precious heat, for outside it was still 600 below and getting colder. The Commander and his men had combed the ice out of their beards and thawed the icicles from their moustaches. They brushed the snow off their boots and stripped off their big steaming parkas; for the first time the fuselage men saw them in white woollen roll neck sweaters.

Soon conversation and laughter filled the Hastings and the steam from their breaths set up a permanent mist. It was the first time any of the eighteen men of Northice had relaxed from the tension of the past five days and it was good to see.

Presently dinner was served. The cooks ladled it out of their primus pots into R.A.F. mess tins and the helpings were passed from hand to hand. Nobody cared that the tins were caked with the remnants of five days' eating. Boyd and Jones had responded magnificently. From probably the coldest kitchen in the world they had produced huge steaming helpings of a stew containing tinned meat, peas, beans and dehydrated vegetables followed by a desert of pears in hot syrup washed down with cups of rich hot cocoa.

Then Ted poured a man-sized tot of whisky into each of the eighteen cups. As they were passed round everybody added hot water. Whether or not it spoiled their whisky was unimportant; without the water it would have frozen in their mouths.

From the far end of the fuselage where he lay in his sleeping-bag beside Frank Burke, whose head was still hurting too much to talk, Smokey called for silence. "Gentlemen," he said, "I think our first toast should be to the Queen." There were murmurs of assent and in that steaming smoke-laden compartment of Her Majesty's coldest aircraft they drank Her health with a sip of warm whisky. The Commander then proposed a toast and they drank to the President of the United States. After that there wasn't enough whisky left for any more toasting, but the 8,000 feet of altitude and the hot water had already given the whisky a boost.

Reg Michie said: "Well Mike, what about a song?" And Mike putting on his richest brogue obliged with a long Irish ditty called "Mary's Ass" in which everybody joined in the chorus. He ended amid cheers and applause gasping for breath. Not only their party but the fuselage had now warmed up. The heat from eighteen bodies made the little survival compartment the warmest it had been since the crash. Angus Erskine with his deep booming voice entertained them with wardroom yarns and songs, Graham Rollitt sang and then Mike unfolded a scries of stories of old Ireland, of his life as a "mercenary" with the R.A.F. and of his own colourful family history which he traced with a string of libellous anecdotes back to the 11th Century.

For several hours all thoughts of their own discomfort and danger were overshadowed by the evening's hilarity. Occasionally above the noise in the fuselage would come the wail of the wind outside and the hiss of snow pouring over the wings; but the moaning orchestra of the ice-cap did little to subdue the spirits within.

The party seemed hardly to have begun when the Commander looked at his watch. It was 10.30. "Mike," he said, "I think we'll be off; the patients look a bit tired." The six explorers pulled on their parkas, thanked their hosts and to avoid cooling down the fuselage slipped away to their tents two by two.

That night Mike decided in view of the unlikelihood of fire at this stage to reduce the night watch to one man. He took the 4 to 6 a.m. turn himself, sitting by the primuses, alone with the whistle of the wind and his own thoughts. Occasionally he peeped through the curtains at the rows of sleeping-bags and from the steam spirals he could see that even after the exhaustion of nearly six days of this life few of the men were yet sleeping. And then he remembered that it was Sunday morning. Back at Topcliffe he would have been stirring himself for early Mass. This would be one of the few Sundays in his life when he had missed the comfort of that.

Outside it was getting light. Mike hoped it would be the last ice-cap dawn he would ever see for this was the day Thule had promised to rescue them. He looked out through the frost crystalled window. It was a hazy morning, the overcast reached right down onto the cap and merged in one grey-white mass with the clouds of wind-blown snow which passed by in sombre marching curtains. It was certainly no weather for rescue. In fact as Mike looked out on this bleak depressing whiteness he began seriously to wonder whether despite Thule's encouraging rescue plans the Greenland weather would ever relent long enough for an aircraft to land and take off from Northice.

The sixth day, September 21, began like every other day with the ritual of the elsan. Because the contents of the portable toilet were perpetually frozen the can had first to be held over the primuses for several minutes before it could be taken outside and emptied. With the temperature at 60° below and the certain consequence of serious burns if flesh came into the barest contact with metal the business of using the elsan had become a major peril. To minimize the risk they used it every morning in quick succession taking elaborate precautions to put several layers of clothing between them and the frigid scat in contortions that would have been highly comical in any but these circumstances.

When it became obvious as the weather deteriorated throughout the morning that there could be no hope of air rescue that day the Herman-Nelson heater became the centre of all interest. But here there was further bitter disappointment. Ted Adair, Corporal Yates and Dick Mosley — he had read the instruction manual from cover to cover several times over — went out to test the machine that could revolutionize their existence, before installing it inside. After a great deal of trouble, constant reference to the Herman-Nelson "bible" and endless manipulation the engine roared to life to the accompaniment of cheering from inside the fuselage. Ten minutes later there was a loud report. Out of a cloud of smoke which hung over the now silent heater came a string of oaths. The crankcase had blown out; apparently it had been damaged in the drop. Their only prospective source of warmth gone the Hastings' men retired dejected to the "fug-hole".

During the day Hastings 490 made an attempt to reach Northice with more supplies. But visibility over the cap was so poor the aircraft abandoned the operation after a fruitless forty minute search. Ken Taylor heard its signals alternately strengthening and fading as it flew about at times quite close, but Northice might not have existed at all that day it was so heavily cloaked in grey arctic overcast.

While he was still talking to the Hastings Ken Taylor received a curious message for Mike. "Please tell Flight Lieutenant Clancy we are sorry but there are no suitable notice boards at Thule," the radio apologized. Mike looked puzzled.

"The devil there aren't," he said. "And what notice boards might these be?"

A ripple of laughter went through the "fug-hole". Mike swung round. Reg and "Richie" couldn't contain themselves. "It was just an idea we had," said Reg grinning. "We thought that with all the orders that have been flying round here we would do the thing properly. We were going to have one notice board inside for the R.A.F. and another outside for the Army. They were to be 'Clancy's Daily Orders'."

Mike had to laugh with the rest of them. He knew he had been giving a lot of orders. But then they were in a situation where orders were vital to survival. He knew, too, that his constant suggestions that they should get out and exercise by supply collecting on the D.Z. had not always met with joyous response. But he understood that because he had deliberately driven himself to exercise more than he needed to, and as a result he felt — with the possible exception of Corporal Yates, the hardest-working man in the fuselage — fitter than anyone else. In fact his excessive energy made him a constant butt of good-humoured leg-pulling from their two principal wits, Reg and "Richie".

Mike was often amused to hear them discussing him in the "fug-hole". If he was in another fuselage compartment the speakers would raise their voices to make sure he heard what they had to say.

A voice would say: "I don't think I'll go out this morning; my chest's in a bad way." And Reg would add: "If Clancy drives us any further we'll have no chests left."

"We were out on the D.Z. this morning," "Richie" would say, "and we saw him in a snow hole. He was digging furiously, snow flying in all directions and we thought, this can't go on, he must drop soon."

Mike would shout through the drapings: "That fug hole will be the death of all of you, to be sure it will." Whereupon Reg would hiss loud enough for Mike to hear: "Keep quiet for heaven't sake or he'll have us all out on the D.Z. doing P.T!"

That Sunday the Commander asked Mike if they would care to join the expedition in a simple religious service. "We usually mark our Sundays in this way," he said. Mike thought it an excellent idea and when he put it to the others they all agreed. Somebody said: "It isn't often I pray but if it'll get us off this ruddy ice-cap I'm willing to stay on my knees all night."

The Commander took the service in the fuselage. It was non-denominational and followed the pattern of that used by the Royal Navy at sea. The six explorers filed quietly into the aircraft and sat themselves down on the sleeping-bags as they had done the night before. But there was a different atmosphere in the fuselage this time. Last night the two parties had gathered to entertain each other, to let off a little steam and to cheer each other up. Tonight the scene was the same: there were the three injured men side by side in their sleeping-bags, Frank Burke with his head bandaged and a grotesque strip of plaster from cheek to cheek across his broken nose, Smokey in his smart U.S.A.F. bag in the middle, and bespectacled Major Barker-Simson-next to him. The same lanterns cast the same soft shadows on the gaudy drapings and the smoky atmosphere was again thick with the breath of eighteen men. It was the same scene but the atmosphere had changed. The common purpose for which they had collected together this time reduced the conversation to a low hush; the boisterous spirit of last night had gone.

It was a brief and moving service and although it lasted barely twenty minutes the impact remained with them all for a long time after. From the pocket of his steaming parka Commander Simpson produced two prayer books. One was a Catholic prayer book which he handed to Mike. And then while they all sat round him, a bearded almost piratical-looking gathering with bowed uncovered heads, the Commander began reading in his firm quiet voice the Collects of Thanksgiving. Then he read the Lesson. It was from St Paul's Epistle to the Corinthians — "though we may speak with divers tongues..." — Together they chanted the Lord's Prayer and the eighteen murmuring voices seemed to merge with the whine of the wind outside. The wind was their only music, the wind and the howl of restless dogs and occasionally the harsh grating of the torn wing tip.

In strange contrast to the precise English accent of the expedition leader, Mike read a short Catholic service in his lilting Irish tones for himself and Frank Burke. And then the Commander ended the service with the sailors' Prayer of Thanksgiving for deliverance after shipwreck. Quietly everybody got to their feet. There were brief goodnights, the six explorers pulled their parka hoods over their heads; silently they filed out through the drapings and into the freezing night. Long after they had gone a feeling of serenity still remained with the men in that grimy miserable fuselage.

That night Smokey gave Mike a bad fright. Mike was on watch at three a.m. when the American called him out of the "fug-hole" with a hoarse urgent whisper. Taking a storm lantern Mike hurried through into the sleeping compartment. There was panic in Smokey's face, a look of fear that Mike hadn't seen there in all the injured man's six days of agony. "Mike," he said, "I think I'm losing the feeling in my feet." Deeply disturbed Mike knelt down beside him. "Let's have a look at them," he said, "one at a time."

Painfully, Smokey drew a leg out of his bag and Mike gently peeled off the felt bootie, three thick woollen socks and one black cotton one. Immediately the bare foot began to steam, furiously. Mike held the lamp near it. He gasped. All colour had drained away leaving the lower part of the foot with a deadly marble-like pallor. There was only one thing that could save Smokey's foot from serious frostbite, and, probably, amputation; Mike did it.

Loosening his own clothing he sat down beside Smokey, clamped his numbed foot against his shirt and rubbed it with bare hands. It sent a cold shock across his chest and by removing his gloves he was inviting frostbite, but it did the trick. Soon Smokey could feel the warmth from Mike's chest seeping into his dead feet and after half an hour of massage there was feeling in all his toes again. Mike quickly replaced the socks and bootie and repeated the performance on the other foot. While he worked he held the socks under his parka. If he hadn't they would have been too stiff to put on again within five minutes in that perishing cold.

When it was all over Smokey's bearded face showed intense relief. "I guess you've saved those durned feet o' mine," he said. "At one time there I really thought they were never going to be a part of me again."

CHAPTER 9

IT WAS now nearly a week since the Hastings had crashed on the ice-cap. And throughout the world where the "Marooned Fliers" were still making headlines the same question was being asked over and over again: "Why doesn't somebody rescue them?".

Rescue, however, was not quite the simple business it may have sounded several thousand miles away. The major operation of landing on the ice-cap and picking up the twelve men had in fact been occupying the minds both of the Air Ministry and the U.S.A.F. for six days. But it was not a task that could be hurried. No 6 Air Rescue Squadron, U.S.A.F., which was preparing for the operation at Thule was breaking new and hazardous ground attempting a landing more than a mile and a half above sea level. The Hastings was higher than they had ever landed before. It was also a long way — 480 miles — from Thule and there was the risk that if the rescue aircraft were delayed on the cap and weather deteriorated on the coast it might not be able to get back as the nearest diversion airfields in southern Greenland were beyond the range of the ski-wheeled Dakota with which it was planned to make the rescue. As it was unlikely that the aircraft would succeed in getting off snow at 8,500 feet with a load of passengers the whole success of the operation depended on the use of JATO — jet assisted take-off. This was a rocket device which added tremendous power to the take-off for a few seconds — long enough to get an aircraft off a very short runway in a fraction of the distance its engines would take unaided, or, in the case of the ice-cap long enough to overcome the lack of take-off power caused by the rarefied air and get the aircraft well into the air where its own engines could cope.

There was also the problem of navigation. The rescue aircraft wouldn't have the fuel to spare for a long search for Northice. It had to be flown out from Thule and back in a straight line. This meant positioning other aircraft along the route to give the rescue pilot radio navigation assistance.

At Thule the rescue was in very capable hands. It was being planned by some of the U.S.A.F.'s most experienced Arctic experts who had been doing little else for nearly a week. They included famous Colonel Bernt Balchin, the U.S.A.F's. Norwegian-born Arctic Adviser, Lt.-Col. John Nichols, officer commanding, 6 Air Rescue Squadron and Colonel Humphreys, the Base Commander. Squadron Leader Robinson, the Hastings detachment commander represented the R.A.F. at planning conferences; later the R.A.F. were to send a senior Transport Command officer, Group Captain Kennedy as a rescue liaison officer. He flew to Thule in a Hastings, captained by Flight Lieutenant Bailey, which replaced the crashed aircraft on the airlift to Northice. The same aircraft brought Captain Luty and three more Army despatchers to replace the despatches stranded on the cap.

Although the Hastings men had been promised rescue on Sunday, September 21, bad weather had delayed the assembly of the aircraft that were to take part. In fact the ski-Dakota did not arrive at Thule until the 22nd. As it then had to be stripped of all unnecessary weight and specially prepared for the operation it was decided that the Rescue Squadron's S.A. 16, a twin-engined Grumman Albatros amphibian should attempt to land at Northice and take off the three injured men; three was the maximum number of passengers the Albatross could safely take off with at 8,500 feet. It was hoped that the Dakota, which could take off from the same height with nine passengers, would be ready to rescue the rest of the men the following day.

A bevy of supporting aircraft was standing by at Thule to help the two rescue planes. A Flying Fortress was to fly out a third of the way to Northice and circle there transmitting homing signals. A second Fortress was to do the same thing two-thirds of the way out. Over the scene of the crash a Skymaster was to act as control aircraft; Colonel Balchin and a parachute rescue team were to fly in it, the former to offer on-the-spot-advice, the latter to jump if they were needed. David Wright's Hastings was to help, too. After making a routine supply drop at Northice it was to orbit to give radio homing assistance while a fifth aircraft, another Flying Fortress, was to escort the rescue aircraft on their flight out and back.

In the bleak fuselage at Northice on Monday the 22nd nobody knew of these lavish plans. With the temperature now down to 64° below, most of them spent a miserable day in their sleeping-bags.

Just in case the rescue planes came, a working party went out onto the runway and cleared the snow off the parachute markers. The Hastings came out and dropped a load of supplies but all enthusiasm for this event had gone. Ted Adair summed it up in the log that afternoon: "Nobody is keen on digging the loads out any more, as it is a very tedious and difficult job."

The most talked of event of the day was the appearance of a small bird. Blue and white coloured it was first seen flitting from one pile of stores to another and was immediately the subject of much speculation. The ice-cap supports no natural life and it seemed problematical that such a tiny bird — it was no bigger than a sparrow — could have flown from either coast. The Commander had the most likely theory. He said it must have come from Thule trapped in one of the parachute loads. However, after that afternoon Northice's smallest visitor was never seen again.

There were several people at R.A.F. Topcliffe who at the end of the Hasting's first week on the ice-cap would gladly have changed places with them. The station was besieged with inquiries from morning till night. Anxious relatives of the stranded men wrote and telephoned — "when is my boy going to be rescued?"... "are you *sure* he will be warm enough?" — total strangers rang to ask for the latest news and a company of reporters had firmly entrenched themselves in the district collecting titbits of information on the men in the fuselage from their friends and families.

The man from Harrogate wrote again sending the R.A.F. details "for possible future use" of an air-insulated snow tent. He enclosed diagrams of the tent marked "confidential" because, he wrote, "any firm making it would probably do the development work if there was an arrangement for a joint patent".

Flight Lieutenant Harben replied: "... I have placed your second letter on an arctic file where it will be readily available for reference should the necessity occur in the future. I would like to add how gratifying it is to feel that such a close bond of mutual esteem and consideration exists between the local populace and ourselves of R.A.F. Topcliffe".

September 23, their seventh day on the cap began as just another morning for the Hastings men; but when the pale orange sun sank below the grey rim of the horizon that evening only nine men remained in the fuselage and a small amphibian aircraft had made aviation history.

A radio report at eight a.m. that a plane was on the way brought temporary excitement only matched by the gloom which followed Ken Taylor's announcement that it was only the faithful Hastings making yet another supply drop. With the temperature now down to — 35° — 67° of frost — it had become so cruelly cold that even the "fug-hole" with its two belching primuses and its close hung drapings offered very little relief. The inside of the aircraft was caked with frost and the air so cold that whenever anyone spoke his condensing breath almost obscured him in the local fog he created.

After lunch Ken Taylor made contact with the Hastings. Suddenly he shouted from his little compartment the news for which they had been hoping and praying for seven days: "There's a rescue kite on the way, lads — a small flying-boat. He's coming to try and get the injured off." A cheer went through the fuselage and all the discomfort of the last miserable week was forgotten in a babble of discussion. Only Smokey lay silent in his sleeping-bag. He alone knew of the limitations of the S.A.16, knew that it had never landed and taken off at such a height before and knew that in attempting to do so its pilot was gambling with safety.

Presently came the drone of an aircraft. Everybody rushed outside. For the ice-cap it was a fine day. Overhead the sky showed powder-blue through the sparkling crystals of ice haze; visibility was three miles and the glare off the snow was so dazzling that those who had neglected to bring their snow goggles went reeling back semi-blinded to look for them. It was the Hastings and after it had littered the dropping zone with another consignment of expedition stores it remained over Northice circling so that its radio could guide the rescue plane in.

Inside the fuselage Ted Adair and Corporal Yates prepared the three patients for their journey. Smokey was still suffering badly from his fractured vertebrae — although then nobody knew for certain what his injuries were — Frank Burke's head still throbbed and he winced every time a door was opened or closed; most fortunate of all was Major Barker-Simson whose ankle had been so effectively bandaged by Ted he had lately been able to hop about the fuselage. Now he was made comfortable in his sleeping-bag again.

Six hundred yards behind the tail of the Hastings, Mike and the others hurriedly prepared the runway. Mike appointed himself runway controller and stood at the end of the runway by the parachute pyramid marking the touch-down point. His equipment was a cowling full of frozen oil, a Very pistol and cartridges and a big orange fluorescent panel which he draped over his shoulders so the pilot would see him His beard matted with ice, his parka hood drawn over his head and the brilliant orange panel fluttering from his shoulders he looked like some curious Arctic high priest at the altar.

Away to the west came the noise of an aircraft, faintly at first but growing louder. Three aircraft loomed out of the haze. One was the twin-engined Grumman Albatross the others were a Flying Fortress and a Skymaster. The Fortress had kept close to the Albatross throughout the 480-mile flight out from Thule using its greater radio navigational equipment to guide the smaller aircraft. The Skymaster, carrying an American parachute rescue team and Colonel Balchin, was the director aircraft supervising the whole operation. With the Hastings circling nearby there were now four planes orbiting the derelict British aircraft on the snow; between Northice and Thule another two Fortresses having helped the rescue group out were waiting respectively 160 and 320 miles from Thule to guide them safely home again.

Angus Erskine four feet down inside a snow hole recovering a parachute load looked up, rubbed the steam off his goggles and, shouting to make himself heard above the noise overhead, said to Mike: "It used to be such a peaceful spot but it's getting more like London Airport every day."

Mike set alight to the oil, but as before it produced a useless white smoke so he fired a red Very in the landing direction. The Albatross, silver with red markings on its wings and tail and the big reassuring word RESCUE painted on the forward part of the fuselage made a wide sweep. Its pilot, Major Harold Julin, then flew down the runway between the parachute markers a few feet above the snow. He lowered his hull almost onto the surface to get the feel of this makeshift runway then opened his throttles and swept round for another 'touch and go" run. Twice the Major made a dummy run and then on his third approach he put the amphibian gently down into the snow on its hull. Immediately it disappeared from view in a huge cloud of snow which showered around it as the broad surface of the hull cut a long trench a yard wide and two feet deep. The R.A.F. men gasped. Landing flying-boats or amphibians on their hull on any other medium than water was something they had never considered possible. But there in front of their very eyes it had been done neatly and safely.

Now the Albatross was taxiing quickly across to the crashed aircraft, a flurry of snow billowing behind it. It had small extension skis hanging down from the floats and slid over the dry powdery surface with remarkable ease. A few yards behind the Hastings it stopped, but Major Julin kept his engines ticking over. Had he stopped them he might never have started them again in that intense cold. A door opened and a man jumped out. He was Lieutenant H. C. Holden one of 6 Air Rescue Squadron's parachute medical officers. He hurried across to the Hastings.

"Where are the wounded?" he said, blinking in the gloom of the fuselage. Someone led him through the frozen curtains of coloured silk to the three sleeping-bags each with a bearded expectant face at the top.

"Who's Stover?" demanded Holden. Smokey said: "Are you the doc?" and Holden replied "Yeah, I'm the doc. How are you Stover?"

Smokey said "I'm having a pretty rough time".

Thirty minutes later the three casualties were in litters aboard the Albatross. The nine men whose turn, they hoped, would be next shouted cheery farewells and Frank Burke, all too conscious of the risk he was about to take called to Mike: "Just in case we don't make it — see my wife when you get back".

Meanwhile the rescue pilot and his co-pilot, Captain Woodrow Gilbert, were struggling to fit the 200-lb JATO cylinders to give them the extra kick they needed to get off the snow. The heavy cumbersome steel bottles had to be attached to brackets by the port and starboard hatch doors. It was a tricky job at the best of times but at 67 below with the freezing blast of the slipstream from the idling motors whipping snow into their faces, trying to make intricate adjustments with several layers of gloves and prevented by the altitude from normal exertion it was an exhausting and acutely difficult operation. It took nearly half an hour to get the port cylinder on and then they found to their horror that the starboard release gear was not functioning properly. Unless it was fixed they couldn't take off. Dick Mosley hurried into the fuselage and returned with his flight engineer's tool kit to lend a hand.

But the faulty mechanism at first defied all efforts to fix it. It was an hour and a half after the Albatross had landed before Major Julin was satisfied that his JATO gear was safe to use. He had planned to spend only twenty minutes on the snow; if he was to have enough fuel left for the return flight he would have to get off immediately. Overhead the Hastings, Fortress and Skymaster were still circling and waiting while agitated American voices on the radio inquired "What the hell goes on down there, Julin?".

In the cockpit Major Julin was strapping himself in for the take-off. Somebody tapped him on the shoulder. He looked round to see a heavily bearded face etched with chunks of ice. The man held a book and a pen in his gloved hands. He handed them to the Major who was astonished to hear him yell above the noise of the motors, "Would you mind signing please?" It was Graham Rollitt collecting signatures for Northice's visitors' book. The crew of the rescue plane brought his total to an impressive twenty-one.

The door was slammed shut and they all stood back a few yards. Nearby Commander Simpson watched anxiously. But the ice-cap does not let aircraft leave its sticky frigid surface easily. When Major Julin opened up his throttles to taxi away the amphibian wouldn't move. He tried full power, power on alternate engines, on both engines together, full power on one and reverse pitch on the other. It was no use; the amphibian had frozen hard onto the snow. Those watching looked at each other glumly. Were another aircraft and three more men to join the little colony of the marooned? Things looked serious.

The pilot closed the throttles and Captain Gilbert came out. He climbed onto the port float and rocked the wing. Ted Adair and Corporal Yates seized snow shovels and began furiously digging snow away from the frozen hull. Again the engines roared; nothing happened. It was now an hour and forty minutes since the aircraft touched down. Its engines had been ticking over all that time and soon it wouldn't have enough fuel left to make Thule.

Lying anxiously in their litters aboard the aircraft the three injured men began to have fearful thoughts. The warmth, the clean sheets and the hospital attention they wanted more than anything had seemed so close an hour ago. Now they seemed remoter than ever. From the cockpit they could hear the voice of Colonel Balchin in the Skymaster above. It came through in shouted staccato snatches on the radio — words of advice from a man who knew better than anyone just what to do.

They heard Major Julin's irate voice saying, "I can't shift her" and the Colonel's accented reply "Viggle the vings, Julin, viggle the vings." And despite their impatience and anxiety they chuckled when the radio brought Julin's exasperated answer, "I've *wiggled* them" and the immediate retort from above, "Then viggle them again!"

Blue with cold, Captain Gilbert was still rocking. As he swayed the aircraft Major Julin juggled with the throttles desperately trying to twist the Albatross even a few inches. And then suddenly the plane gave a jerk and lurched forward. Gilbert leapt down off the float and into the cabin. But he was too late. As the pilot had reduced power to let him aboard, the hull had refrozen. The situation was desperate.

"Richie" decided to have a shot at rocking. The others helped him up onto the float and he heaved it up and down. Again the engines screamed, the freezing blast nearly flung him off his perch but somehow he managed to hang on. The amphibian shuddered, moved a few inches, stopped, then moved forward again, several feet this time. But before Captain

Gilbert, who had come out again, could get back, it had stopped. "Richie" slid down, exhausted.

Now Mike climbed up and Gilbert went aboard. The procedure was repeated. And then, wonderful moment, the Albatross began to crawl forward. This time Major Julin didn't stop. He knew better. Slowly it gathered speed. At first Mike didn't realize that it couldn't stop to let him off and he stayed there. But when he found that he was being carried out to the take-off point he quickly let go and rolled into the snow. (Later at Thule Major Julin told Mike: "I would have taken off with you on the god-darned float and flown you back to Thule. Nothing would have made me stop that little ship once she started moving").

In a silent group they stood there, the six men of the expedition and the nine Hastings men. They watched the Albatross drag itself out to the take-off point. It seemed to be moving painfully slowly. Then, 600 yards away they heard the engines roar at full throttle. Immediately the aircraft was lost in a huge swirling cloud of snow. For the onlookers this was the worst moment of all. Inside that moving snow cloud a silver and red aeroplane was attempting something that had never been done before. For an eternity it seemed to stay on the surface. Surely it should be airborne by now.

Suddenly the snow crust shook. Although the wind carried the roar of the jets away from them the men on the ground knew the pilot had fired his JATO's. For fully half a minute they scanned the horizon where the big snow cloud still hung; there was no sight nor sound of the amphibian.

And then they saw it, five miles away, a tiny silhouette rising out of the haze into the setting sun. The operation had succeeded. It was a moment of intense relief. Mike looked at the Commander. His face was still tense and on each cheek there was a small tear. "Thank God", was all he said. And Mike knew how he meant it.

CHAPTER 10

AFTER the powerful thrust of the JATO's had swung them safely into the sky fresh trouble awaited the men in the rescue amphibian. Soon after they had rejoined the waiting Fortress, Thule radioed that bad weather was closing in on the coast. For Major Julin this was serious news. It was a three hour flight back to Thule and after the delay on the snow he now had barely three and a half hours' fuel left in his tanks. He certainly had no margin for a diversion elsewhere; it was imperative that he made base before it was blotted out by low cloud and snow showers.

And then the amphibian's heating system packed up. Within a few minutes all warmth in the cabin had gone. It became so bitterly cold that the injured men, unable to move in their litters began to lose the feeling in their limbs. Most seriously affected was Major Barker-Simson. His feet went dead; without some warmth they could have been seriously frostbitten in a very short time.

The Major's feet were saved by the gallant action of the American flight doctor. Despite the intense cold he himself was feeling, Lieutenant Holden loosened his clothing and gripped Barker-Simson's feet against the warmth of his bare chest. For the long three hours of the flight back to Thule he held them there while the Major felt the circulation slowly ebbing back. Today he owes his feet to that unselfish gesture of the "paramedic".

A hundred miles from Thule the Albatross was running perilously low in fuel; the weather was deteriorating almost as quickly. Fearing that Major Julin might have to force land on the ice-cap short of his destination Thule ordered a Flying Fortress to stand by with drums of emergency fuel. If needed, it would fly out and parachute the fuel down, the crew would refuel and if the weather at Thule was still safe for a landing the amphibian would take off and continue the flight. A hundred miles from Thule the cap had sloped down to only 4,000 feet above sea level and the Albatross could attempt a take-off without JATO.

Fortunately the plan was unnecessary. On the fringe of an approaching blizzard the amphibian crept in over the edge of the inland ice, in the gathering dusk its big wheels swung down and a few minutes later it crunched onto Thule's long crushed rock runway. It had just thirty minutes' fuel left. Shortly afterward the other aircraft whose radio navigational assistance had made the operation possible also touched down. They were only just in time. Even while the three casualties were being carried into Thule's modern hospital a fierce blizzard had begun to howl around the low aluminium buildings and the airfield was closed for all flying. The air rescue squadron had gambled — and succeeded, but only just.

Back in the fuselage at Northice nine men had a problem. The Albatross had left them four JATO cylinders to store in the fuselage in case the second rescue aircraft needed them. "Keep these little bottles warm; keep em above freezing temperature", the amphibian pilot had warned as he handed them over. Perhaps he thought the R.A.F. had devised some Thule-style steam heating at Northice. All metal on the ice-cap was frozen and stayed that way. Even if their rescue depended on it they wouldn't have been able to keep four big steel cylinders anything near freezing. As somebody remarked, "It'd be difficult enough trying to keep these things above minus forty". However they did their best with them, storing them in the "fug-hole" wrapped in parachutes and feeling distinctly uneasy about the presence of such highly inflammable stores.

The fuselage looked empty without the three casualties. They looked wistfully at the end of the sleeping-compartment where the long suffering trio had lain side by side for a week and hoped that it wouldn't be long before the radio told them the Albatross had safely reached Thule.

Meanwhile to cheer them up there were mail and newspapers from home. The Hastings had dropped them in a bag with a long red streamer attached, and now they crowded into the fetid atmosphere of the "fug-hole" to devour messages from wives and mothers and Press interpretations of their predicament. There was a letter for Mike cryptically addressed "MIKE, ICE CAP". He ripped it open. It was from his wife. "Darling", she wrote, "Please don't worry about us; we are not worrying about you". He smiled; just like Cecilia to make light of it all.

As they opened the newspapers they realized for the first time how wide was public interest in their situation. They stared in horror at photographs of themselves taken years before which enterprising news editors had borrowed from their families. Somebody groaned, "Just look what my mother's been saying to the newspapers", and someone else interrupted with "Get a load of this. It says here the R.A.F. is going to dismantle the Hastings and sledge it *piece by piece* to the coast!" This ludicrous suggestion was only capped by another colourful bit of speculation which suggested that with the movement of the inland ice the Hastings would one day be delivered safely on the coast, 250 miles away. Mike did a rough calculation. "I hope the R.A.F. will still want old 492 in ten million years", he said.

The amphibian had brought them a welcome addition to their larder — two 50-lb slabs of fresh steak. Their mouths watered at the sight of it. Wrapped in a muslin bag it was frozen as hard as marble. Someone tried cutting it with an axe: the blade just bounced off, dislodging only a pebble of hard meat which tinkled onto the floor. Ken Taylor on his way to the radio compartment looked in. "I'll have a look in the carpenter's kit", he said. He came back with a tenon saw. Mike began sawing. A quarter of an hour later watched by eight pairs of hungry eyes he was still frantically sawing and had only made a cut a paltry inch deep. The trouble was that the friction melted the grease, the grease immediately refroze and clogged the saw. Somebody suggested heating the blade. It proved to be sound Arctic butchery technique. After a few seconds in the primus flame the saw sank into the meat as easily as if it were butter. Soon a stack of generous slices was sizzling in the pan. It was the finest meal they had eaten for a week; they could almost feel the steak coursing through their systems putting fresh life into them.

Just before they turned in for the night Ken Taylor yelled from the radio room: "They made it, lads; the three of them are safe in hospital at Thule". The tension which all of them had been feeling but trying not to show ever since the amphibian faded away to the west was now lifted from them. For a long time they just sat, each silent with his own thoughts. Ted broke the spell. "Thank God for that", he said quietly.

It was colder than ever that night, colder because they had lost the heat of three bodies, colder because the temperature had crept down still further. There seemed no limit to the depths to which the temperature could drop. It seared mercilessly through the metal fuselage, through the frosty drapings, through every layer of clothing. Long ago they had forgotten what it felt like to be even comfortably warm. That night they rearranged the parachute curtains, contracting the sleeping-quarters in a vain effort to make sleep possible.

But it was too miserably cold; they had almost forgotten, too, what normal unbroken sleep meant. Their nights had become miserable ordeals in which few of them slept except in brief disturbed snatches when through sheer physical exhaustion they dozed until the cruel stabbing cold brought them back to wakefulness.

Their eighth ice-cap dawn brought a revival of hope. This was to be their last day at Northice; this was rescue day. The midday radio contact with Britannia Lake brought promising news. The Hastings was on the way with another supply load and, wonderful news, a ski-wheeled Dakota would be following it. This, at last, they thought, was it.

With feverish excitement they prepared for the exodus. They pulled on every spare bit of clothing they could find, cooked what they thought was their last fuselage meal and tramped out to the runway to clear the night's snow off the coloured markers and moved the whole runway fifty yards to one side so that the Dakota wouldn't have to land in the trench the amphibian's hull had cut the previous day. And then came the anti-climax.

The Hastings arrived overhead and radioed down the disappointing news that the Dakota wouldn't be coming after all. Rescue had been postponed.

It was a bitter blow. Silently they trooped back to the "fughole" to commiserate round the primuses. Ken Taylor said: "Bad news, lads; duff weather at Thule. They say they'll try tomorrow". One of the soldiers asked incredulously: "If the weather's all that bad can somebody tell me why the Hell the Hastings is here?".

Mike explained that it was probably a question of range. The Hastings carried enough fuel to divert to another base if the weather closed in behind it on the coast. The Dakota wouldn't have the range to do this particularly as it would be returning with a greater payload. An important condition of its mission, therefore, was sufficiently clear weather to permit a direct flight to and from Northice.

Despite his assurances, however, Mike had private misgivings that there might be another reason behind the postponement. Perhaps, he thought, Thule was not immediately willing to risk a recurrence of the first aircraft's failure to get off when it froze onto the snow. That night as he lay in his sleeping-bag listening to the sleepless gruntings of his colleagues and the asthmatical wheezing of the wind outside he wondered if after all they mightn't have to make the overland sledge journey they had all been dreading. But his fears were groundless.

Thursday, September 25, was their ninth, coldest, and last day on the snow. When Commander Simpson made his morning visit to the fuselage he was able to tell them the temperature was exactly minus forty degrees — 72°F below freezing. They breakfasted on cereal and hot milk, fried bread and bacon. It was cold almost as soon as it left the primus and it stuck in a glutinous mess to the fatty remnants of eight days' meals which had almost become a part of the bottom of their mess tins. But nobody cared after Ken Taylor, the medium of all their hopes and disappointments, called from the radio just two words: "They're coming".

This time there was no doubt about it. The weather was clear with the best visibility for several days. Five miles away the grey line of the horizon shimmered and danced in the watery morning sunshine. Outside the fuselage, now banked high with a week's drifting snow, the nine men stood, backs to the freezing wind, in an excited chattering group. This was their most cheerful hour.

The Hastings came first, around midday, for a routine drop. It told them that Thule's rescue machinery was again in operation: a ski-Dakota escorted by a Flying Fortress and a Skymaster had already left the coast. They were due at Northice at 2.15 p.m.

But at 2.15 there was no sign of the rescue planes, nor by 2.30, nor by 2.45. The nine men anxiously scanned the horizon. If the Dakota didn't arrive soon they wouldn't be able to risk frostbite out in the wind much longer. Already their faces muffled in "dishcloth" scarves were getting the strange numb feeling that they didn't belong to them.

Then at 3 o'clock the Hastings — it had now been circling for three hours — reported that it was going to make a sweep toward Thule to try and make radio contact with the American aircraft. A few minutes later the Hastings was talking to the Flying Fortress and guiding it to Northice. To help the Dakota and its escort find the small pinpoint on the snow the Fortress pilot climbed to 8,000 feet above the cap where his four engines made a fluffy white vapour trail in the hazy blue sky.

Twenty minutes later the Skymaster arrived — but no Dakota. The Dakota had become detached from its escort in the haze and overflown Northice a few miles to the north. Immediately the Hastings flew off toward the north-east in pursuit. Soon it was only a speck in the haze; just before it disappeared they saw a succession of red, green and orange Verys curving away from it. The Dakota pilot, Captain Francis Burnette, saw the flares. Quickly he turned toward the Hastings. A few minutes later the men on the snow saw two specks returning and presently Captain Burnette's voice came up on Ken Taylor's radio. He asked the nine men to wait for him beside the touchdown point and added: "Tell them to come aboard only in the clothes they're standing in and they'd better not be standing in too much. I want as little weight as possible on board for the take-off".

As the Dakota pilot banked low for a look at the snow surface the Hastings' men said good-bye to their hosts of the British North Greenland Expedition. Not for £10,000 would any of them have changed places with these modern Arctic Elizabethans, yet now the time had come to go they suddenly felt a strange sadness. In their struggle for survival a tremendous unselfish spirit of camaraderie had grown up between the two parties and now in a few moments this brief encounter would be over.

Sheltering from the wind in the lee of the fuselage they stood in the snow, fifteen men almost unidentifiable with their parka hoods drawn round their bearded sun-reddened faces. One after the other they gripped heavily gloved hands.

Mike said to the Commander: "It's going to be a huge relief to you to have us off your hands" but the expedition leader replied: "That's not important, Mike. What is important is that you all get safely to Thule. I feel in a way that it's all been my fault. But for me this would never have happened." But Mike assured him that that was so much Blarney. It had been all in the day's work. In supply dropping on the icecap there had been an inevitable element of risk; in their case it had been bad luck.

Graham Rollitt fished in the folds of his parka and produced his visitors' book. Grinning, he said: "Well chaps, the hotel service probably wasn't up to much but just the same would you all mind leaving your mark on the cap." They signed, standing there in the snow steadying the book on each others backs, scribbling their signatures with big scrawling strokes. Rollitt's visitors' book was one of his proudest possessions.

The Dakota flew once up the runway at 400 feet, came quickly round again and landed a few feet from the touchdown indicator, its big skis — a few inches of wheel protruded through them for landing on normal hard runway surfaces — sending a miniature blizzard of loose snow exploding into the air. For nearly a minute the aircraft was lost inside the swirling white shower which followed it along the snow. And then it reappeared taxiing quickly back on the far side of the runway markers, its skis riding smoothly over the hard ripples of the *sastrugi*. Facing into wind it stopped at the start of the runway, ready for the take-off.

With memories of their experience with the amphibian, Mike shouted. "Get aboard quick." The nine of them ran across to the aircraft, wrenched open the door and scrambled panting, inside. Mike closed the door, bolted it tight and they all sat down fastening safety belts for the take-off. This was it, they thought. In less than a minute they would be airborne. But nothing happened.

Instead the door from the crew compartment opened and Captain Burnette, a small middle-aged man with a genial smile, stood there, hands on hips. He gazed with astonishment at his anxious bearded passengers looking like nine desperate brigands in the half light of the cabin. "Dammit boys, but you're quick", he said.

There was no panic around Captain Burnette. Many times before had he landed on the Arctic snow. That this take-off was to be from a record height for a Dakota was no reason for haste.

"Who's Clancy?" he asked.

"I am," said Mike.

"Right Clancy, see those two drums of fuel over there —
we've gotta get all that gas into our tanks."

Mike had noticed the two big fifty-gallon drums lashed inside
the cabin. But it hadn't immediately occurred to him that the
Dakota was to be refuelled.

"And," the Captain was saying, "we've also gotta fix four
little JATO bottles underneath."

The passengers undid their safety belts and lent a hand.
Captain Burnette switched off the port motor, climbed out
onto the port wing and they passed the fuel hose from one of
the drums out to him through a window. It took ten minutes
fierce jerking of a rotary hand pump to empty the drum. Then
the co-pilot, the only other crew member, Lieutenant Alan
Hale, restarted the port motor and turned off the starboard
while the performance was repeated on the other wing tank.
Ted Adair to whom Smokey had lent a magnificent U.S.A.F.
down-filled, fur-lined jacket and who was as a result better able
to face the freezing wind, went out onto the starboard wing to
help.

Meanwhile crouched under the fuselage Captain Burnette
and several R.A.F. volunteers were clamping on the four JATO
cylinders. The wind flung stinging handfuls of snow in their
faces and the cylinders were so cold they seemed to burn their
hands even through their gloves. Quite the most unpleasant
task of the whole rescue, it was accompanied by a withering
torrent of Anglo-American profanity.

The hero of the JATO operation was Flying Officer
Richardson. Struggling with the jet firing mechanism he began
to lose the feeling in his fingers. He took off his gloves and
quickly planted his bare hands under the armpits inside his
parka. But as he held them there trying to squeeze life back
into them there was a shout and one of the 200-lb cylinders

began to slip from its bracket. Richardson was nearest. With thoughts only for the precious bottle he grabbed at it with bare hands. Immediately he yelled in agony. At 72° below, the bottle was as dangerously cold as if it had been red hot. His fingers stuck to the metal and when he pulled them away, strips of skin were glued to the cylinder and his finger-tips were raw and frostbitten.

At last the refuelling was completed, the empty drums pushed out onto the snow, and the JATO cylinders securely locked in position. Everybody climbed aboard. The Commander and his men shouted final farewells and Captain Burnette closed the door. Unhurriedly as though this risky take-off was something he did every afternoon he briefed his passengers.

"Now you guys, there's nothing funny about this JATO business so long as you're all well braced and securely strapped in. First of all I'll open up the motors; you'll feel her rock a bit on the main skis. Then when she's moving and our speed's built up to around thirty to thirty-five miles an hour I'll fire the JATO's. There'll be a bit of a bang, you'll have to hang on to your straps and then before you know what's happened we'll be in the air. Okay, any questions?"

There were none. They were all completely in the hands of Captain Burnette, his Dakota, and the power of the four grey cylinders beneath them.

Captain Burnette disappeared into the crew compartment and closed the door. Tensely they waited for the first shudder that would assure them they were moving and not frozen onto the snow.

Minutes crawled by. The twin motors continued to idle healthily, the three escorting aircraft circled impatiently overhead but the Dakota did not move. The men in the cabin exchanged anxious glances. Why this delay?

And then it was explained. The crew compartment door opened and to their astonishment out came Graham Rollitt clutching his visitors' book. "Sorry chaps," he apologized, "but I had some more signatures to collect."

The motors were coughing open now, the Dakota was rocking on its big ski blades. They were moving. They hadn't stuck after all.

Through the windows they caught a last glimpse of the explorers. They were standing in the snow, six rather lonely-looking figures. Some of them were waving. Behind them lay the derelict outline of the Hastings, the two conical tents, the framework of the hut, a neat pile of stores and a group of dogs, heads back giving vent to howls that were drowned by the noise of the engines. It was their last glimpse of Northice.

Under their feet the JATO's cracked to life. A tremendous roar filled the cabin. Outside the *sastrugi* began to hurtle by. Suddenly the whole white top of the ice-cap sank abruptly away. Their straps tightened on their laps and they rose into the air as though plucked by some unseen hand.

For twenty seconds the roar of the JATO's pressed heavily on their eardrums, swamping the noise of the motors. Suddenly the noise stopped and there was silence. An anguished voice said: "God, the motors have cut". Their hearts stood still. Anxiously they strained their ears for a sound of the engines. There was no sound. They shifted uneasily in their seats — waiting.

And then Mike twisted round and looked out of the windows. The sun shone through the spinning propellers. The engines *hadn't* stopped. Their noise had been momentarily drowned by the thunder of the jets.

"It's all right," said Mike, "you can breathe again."

Far below the ice-cap faded into hazy oblivion. Their nine day's ordeal was over. They were going home.

EPILOGUE

EIGHT months has now passed since Hastings 492 plunged onto the ice-cap. In that time the face of Northice has changed. The little hut in which Graham Rollitt and Ken and Peter Taylor have spent a lonely winter, linked to the outside world only by their radio, has been blanketed in snow. Only the chimneys show that it is there at all. A few yards away the aircraft too is being slowly buried; soon the restless shifting snow of the cap will engulf it for ever.

But at least for another year its cold fuselage will know the tread and sound of man. The British North Greenland Expedition has built a snow tunnel from the aircraft to their hut. It is an ill wind that blows nobody any good; they are using it as a store-house and workshop and have stripped some of its instruments for their own use. One piece of equipment, an air-miles-per-gallon-unit is now at Britannia Lake. The expedition's doctors have converted it into a "blood machine", a device for taking blood counts of samples taken for medical records from members of the team.

Before Commander Simpson, Dr Hamilton and Angus Erskine sledged back to Britannia Lake in mid-October — their dogs had been strengthened for the journey by emergency meat supplies dropped — R.A.F. Hastings aircraft completed the supply drop and one Hastings piloted by Flying Officer Iddison made a long flight from Thule and back to drop mail and rations to members of the expedition on the east coast. In all, Transport Command Hastings flew 86½ tons of supplies in support of the expedition. By wartime supply dropping standards it was a mere drop in the ocean but in view of the previously untried conditions under which the crews operated, the incalculable weather of the ice-cap and the difficulty of finding such a small pinpoint in the world's biggest ice desert and of accurately gauging heights above it at low level it was a courageously successful operation.

After their rescue the Hastings men spent several days at Thule catching up on lost sleep, revelling in the taste of fresh food and adjusting themselves to living again without fighting inescapable cold. Thule's doctors found that all except the injured were none the worse for their ice-cap sojourn and all including Frank Burke and Major Barker Simson fit to return to England.

In the officers' mess at Thule there is a juke box. In the four days the R.A.F. men were there after their rescue the Americans played one record over and over again. The record? A catchy tune called "Clancy lowered the Boom".

A relief Hastings flew the eleven R.A.F. and British Army men back to Topcliffe on a grey October afternoon. They stepped out of the aircraft to face a battery of reporters, photographers, and newsreel cameramen.

Even after their return, Topcliffe continued to receive letters from voluntary advisers and well-wishers. Their biggest fan, the man from Harrogate, wrote again, this time enclosing diagrams of wedge-shaped containers which he hoped the R.A.F. would be able to make use of in building emergency snow survival shelters. Flight Lieutenant Harben replied that his suggestion had been placed on the station's Greenland file.

A Yorkshire girl sent a page from her autograph book for the Hastings men to sign and offered to send them "some very good adventure stories which my brother has read and does not want". She wrote: "I hope you do not mind me writing but I was very impressed by the twelve airmen who were marooned on the Ice-Cap and who are now safely back at their base it must have been an ordeal but they faced it like the British airmen always do cheerful and modest. I am really glad that they are back and I hope you will convey my best wishes to them all. I have always had a big respect for airmen because of my father was an Air Gunner in the war and was killed in 1943. That is why I do not like to hear of such brave men being killed or injured..." She got her autographs but Flight Lieutenant Harben declined her offer of adventure stories. He felt, he wrote, that it would be selfish of the R.A.F. to accept them because they had welfare organizations "which supply us with such comforts and by accepting your offer we might deprive someone less fortunately placed than ourselves". He added: "I am indeed sorry to hear that your father was killed on active service as an Air Gunner. You have good cause to be proud of him as, also, has the Royal Air Force".

Where are the twelve men today? Most of the R.A.F. men are still with 47 Squadron although the Squadron has moved from Topcliffe. Flight Lieutenant Adair, Flight Lieutenant Michie, Flying Officer Richardson — his frostbite was not serious — Master Engineer Mosley and Flight Sergeant Boyd are once again flying Hastings on Transport Command routes. So is Flight Sergeant Burke who has recovered from his head injuries. He is probably the only one of the twelve who can claim to have benefitted physically from the crash. His nose used to be slightly crooked. American doctors who set it after it was broken straightened it for him.

Of the Army despatchers Corporal Yates has been demobbed and is now a civilian again, Corporal Fussey — he has three stripes now — and Private Jones — now a Lance-Corporal — are back at Old Sarum; an inter-Service posting has given their Commander, Major Barker-Simson a post in a transport operations branch of the Air Ministry. His ankle has mended and he is able to walk again.

Mike Clancy who was due for promotion is now a Squadron Leader. His caravan home now rests in a field in the west of England where he is on the staff of the School of Amphibious Warfare. He has had to relate the ice-cap story to reporters, describe it on the radio, demonstrate it in front of television cameras, edify lunch clubs with it and amuse the civic dignitaries of his home town Limerick with survival anecdotes. He doesn't want to see snow again as long as he lives.

It was several months before Smokey Stover fully recovered from his spinal injuries. But after graduating from bed to a wheel chair he was eventually able to walk again and is now back on duty with the U.S.A.F.

One day, ten months after he got back from Greenland, when he had all but forgotten the ice-cap crash, a bundle of fifty letters was dumped in Mike's office. Mostly from women, they came from all parts of the country "to cheer you up in your loneliness". A few days before, the well-meaning but misinformed columnist of a national newspaper had published the photographs of three members of the British North Greenland Expedition and had included Mike's for good measure.

Describing the four as a "group of lonely, lonely men who've had no contact with the world for a year" who "say they want letters more than anything" he invited his readers to get busy and write to them. Letters poured into the Expedition's London headquarters where Mike's share was intercepted and sent to him at the School of Amphibious Warfare.

What do people talk about when they write to an R.A.F. officer they have never met, a man they are told is lonely and hungry for news of the outside world?

They wrote pages about the Coronation, cricket, Everest, the British political scene, the Prime Minister's health, shorter skirts, what they did on Bank Holiday, about their jobs, their gardens, pets, husbands, boy friends, their home towns, the films they had seen, about rationing, their social lives and about their own loneliness. Many of the women detailed their physical measurements; some enclosed snaps of themselves.

A spinster from Leicestershire who said, "I, too, am lonely" told Mike why she had selected him from the four photographs: "It was because you look, well, somehow solid and you have a very placid look about you".

A Northumbrian woman said she was middle-aged, "yearned for the thrill of adventure" and confessed that one of her major problems was that her interests were so much wider than most people's "it is very difficult to have an interesting conversation". From London a girl wrote saying she hoped they hadn't had to kill any animals in Greenland as she was very fond of animals, while a Gainsborough girl warned him of the dangers of Polar bears. "Do take care — they dislike strangers and may kill", she cautioned. A Scots lassie enclosed three photographs of herself, said she had a dog, two pigs, a tortoise, eighty hens and a cat. "I am an old maid", she explained. "My husband", wrote another woman, "has just been demoted from squadron leader to flight lieutenant to do his last three years in the R.A.F. I don't think he likes it very much and think it very unfair. What do you think?" A geographical student picked out Mike because "I have a weakness for the R.A.F." She added: "However, I detest aeroplanes".

"I am no schoolgirl yearning for romance", claimed a Wolverhampton woman, "I am a housewife of eleven years' standing". She had, she said, a "flair for the unconventional" and had once written to a lighthouse keeper — "and a very interesting reply I had too". A nineteen-year-old Barrow-in-Furness girl said: "I am five foot five inches, nine-and-a-half stone, have fair hair, fair complexion, blue eyes and my left eye is a lazy eye". In case Mike was interested she catalogued all the main streets in Barrow, all the cinemas and most of the schools. She was doubtful about giving her address, she said, because "never before have I wrote to anyone like this". But in her last paragraph she relented and gave it.

"My job", wrote a woman from Worcestershire, "is having a narrowing effect on me". She described herself as "female, fair, ten stone four lb, twenty-eight and a schoolteacher". Wistfully another wrote: "I wish I could be with you as I love adventure but being a woman have had, well, practically none".

"Please do not think I am husband-hunting again", said a widow. "I have chosen you because my late husband was in the R.A.F." A Liverpool girl wrote: "You will probably think I am an eligible teenager". But, she hastened to add "I am not. I am twenty-two and work behind the counter of a high-class tea and coffee shop".

An R.A.F. Pilot Officer who had made his first solo the day before wanted to know if Mike had his "wings" as in the newspaper photograph it wasn't very clear. Another man sent three tongue-twisters and some religious tracts and a Royal Navy captain who had met Mike at the School of Amphibious Warfare a few months before expressed surprise that he was now "stuck away in Greenland".

But the letter which Mike prizes most came from the business-canny director of a weaving company in the Outer Hebrides, enclosing a list of woollen goods he could offer. "Dear Sir", it said, "We notice that you are now resident in the

Arctic — vide the Daily — of today's date and enclose price list which may be of interest. Yours faithfully ——"

Guilty at receiving so much fan mail under false pretences, Mike bundled all the letters into a parcel and consigned them to far away Britannia Lake.

As this is written in the summer of 1953 preparations are already being made for the R.A.F. to resupply the British North Greenland Expedition for their second long Arctic winter. Squadron Leader Robinson will command the Thule detachment again and some of the same Hastings crews who flew on the first operations are likely to return to Greenland to drop more stores at Northice where the arrival of weasels has lightened the explorer's task of supply collecting. They will include members of David Wright's crew many of whom were recognized in the Coronation Honours List. And Coastal Command Sunderlands will be there again, too, resuming the airlift in to Britannia Lake. No 201 Squadron, commanded by Squadron Leader R.A.N. McCready, will do the job this time.

Perhaps the finest testimony of the Expedition's gratitude to the men who supplied them from out of the cold Greenland sky came from Commander Simpson. On October 9, a few hours after the last parachute load went floating down to Northice, he sent the following signal to Air Ministry from the ice-cap:

"On the successful completion of the operation please accept the appreciation and thanks of all members of the ice-cap station for the fine job you have done. We realize that the conditions have been novel and difficult and we are extremely sorry that the operation has involved the loss of an aircraft. But without your co-operation the setting up of this station would not have been possible. We are proud to have been

associated with you and your crews in the undertaking and we
hope to see you back over Northice next year. God speed and
happy return".

ACKNOWLEDGEMENTS

This book has been made possible by the generous assistance I have had from officers of the three Services who were associated with the air supplying of the British North Greenland Expedition in the summer of 1952. For information they have given me or for their willingness to check the finished manuscript I am specially indebted to Commander G. Parker, R.N., Wing Commander G. G. N. Barrett, A.F.C. and Bar, Squadron Leader J. Higgins, D.F.C., A.F.C. and Bar, Squadron Leader E. Robinson, O.B.E., Squadron Leader M. A. Clancy, Major D. S. Barker-Simson, Flight Lieutenants A. Yates, E. Adair, R. Michie, Flying Officer L. E. S. J. Richardson, and to all those members of 230 and 47 Squadrons whose suggestions helped to make this book what I hope is an accurate record.

I.M.

A NOTE TO THE READER

If you have enjoyed this book enough to leave a review on **Amazon** and **Goodreads**, then we would be truly grateful.
The Estate of Ian Mackersey

Sapere Books is an exciting new publisher of brilliant fiction and popular history.

To find out more about our latest releases and our monthly bargain books visit our website: **saperebooks.com**